ALBERT EINSTEIN

AND HIS INFLATABLE UNIVERSE

by Dr Mike Goldsmith

Illustrated by Philip Reeve

Scholastic Children's Books,
Euston House, 24 Eversholt Street,
London NW1 1DB, UK

A division of Scholastic Ltd
London ~ New York ~ Toronto ~ Sydney ~ Auckland
Mexico City ~ New Delhi ~ Hong Kong

Published in the UK by Scholastic Ltd, 2001

10 digit ISBN 0 439 99216 8
13 digit ISBN 978 0439 99216 9

Typeset by M Rules
Printed in the UK by CPI Bookmarque, Croydon, CR0 4TD

25 27 29 30 28 26 24

CONTENTS

Everyone's heard of Albert Einstein – he's dead famous. But why?

Lots of people reckon he was the cleverest bloke ever. Maybe he was: how many other people have sorted out so many bits of the Universe? Space, time, atoms, light, gravity, energy ... you name it, Albert had it sussed! Here are just a few of the things Albert found out:

- How the Universe works, and how to stop it deflating.
- How to travel in time.
- How to count atoms.
- How to change things into light and light into things.
- How, if you look really hard up in the sky, you might just be able to see the back of your head.

How did he do all these amazing things? Well, let's have a look in Albert's lost (and – OK – completely imaginary) notebook...

ALBERT'S LOST NOTEBOOK

Memo: how to be the cleverest person ever.

1. Everything in the Universe is really very simple. If it seems a bit complicated, that's just because we're not thinking straight.
2. To work out how the Universe works all you need to do is ask yourself the right questions and think really hard and logically about them. Then you'll be able to work out all sorts of amazing things, but remember...
3. ...don't trust either common-sense answers or what other people say (even if their name is Isaac Newton).

Isaac Newton – he's always popping up when you least expect him. We'll get to him later. Not to mention his law of Universal Gravitation (which Albert showed isn't all that universal after all).

In this book you'll also find out a few things about Albert that might surprise you, like the fact that he was expelled from school, that the Nazis tried to assassinate him, or that he had his brain removed.

Albert's theories deal with things which he couldn't possibly experiment on in a laboratory: things which are incredibly fast, or heavy, or small. So instead of laboratory experiments, he carried out thought experiments, using his amazing imagination to visualize how things like that must behave. Throughout this book, when you come across strange 'what if' questions and investigate the weird and amazing answers you get, you'll be carrying out thought experiments too – often the very same ones Albert did.

Albert used his experiments to uncover the secrets of space and time, like how moving things shrink, how gravity slows down time and how matter bends space. It all sounds totally mind-bending, and people might tell you that you haven't a hope of understanding it all. Well, one of the brilliant things about Albert's theories is that you can follow most of them without any tricky sums. As Albert himself said,

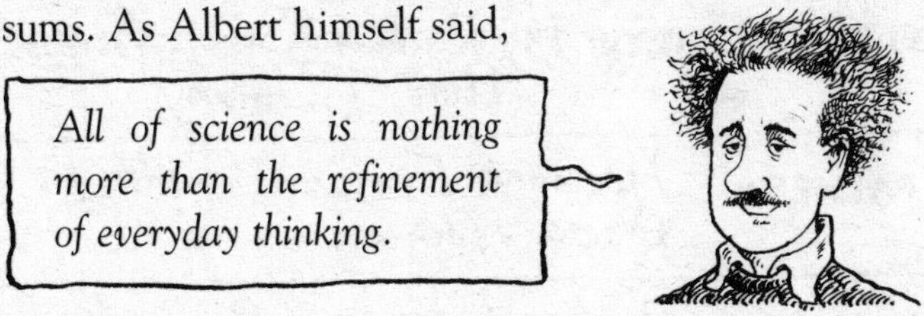

All of science is nothing more than the refinement of everyday thinking.

And this book even has specially prepared fun-sized versions of Albert's theories, to help you get your head round them.

So read on and discover one of the best kept secrets of the 21st century – you *can* understand Albert's theories, it's really not that difficult and it *won't* make your head explode.

THE LITTLE MONSTER

Birth Certificate

NAME: Albert Einstein

DATE OF BIRTH: 11.30 AM, 14 March 1879

PLACE OF BIRTH: 135 Railway Station Street, Ulm, Germany.

FATHER: Hermann Einstein, dealer in Goose feathers.

MOTHER: Pauline Einstein (Pauline Koch before she was married).

DOCTOR'S NOTE: Baby has a weird-shaped head, but is not a monster, whatever his mum says.

When he was born not everybody was wild about poor little Albert's appearance...

Albert was the first genius in his family. But he didn't seem extra clever to begin with. When he first saw his sister, he said…

Albert also learned to talk later than most people, and some people think that's why he developed the vivid visual imagination he used to think about scientific problems. But there was nothing really extraordinary about Albert in those days – he played happily with his sister Maja, and didn't spend his time splitting atoms or anything. But then, when he was about five, Hermann gave him a magnetic compass to play with. Albert was fascinated.

It's hard to imagine being that excited by a compass when you're five: think how much more fun it is to annoy the cat. But Albert wasn't quite like most of us. When he didn't understand something, it upset him and he kept on and on trying to work it out until he'd got it. He was fascinated by magnetism for the rest of his life, though he never quite managed to explain how it fitted into the rest of the Universe.

Another reason Albert got interested in science was his Uncle Jakob. Uncle Jakob was an engineer and also Hermann's business partner, and he told Albert about algebra and geometry and would give him maths problems to solve for fun. Not what everyone would call fun, but Uncle Jakob was great at making things seem like games to Albert, and anyway they couldn't watch TV because it hadn't been invented yet.[1] Albert was to find his early interest in geometry very useful later, when it came to explaining how gravity worked, and he was very impressed to find that in geometry amazing things can be proved by simple step-by-step logical reasoning – just the sort of reasoning he would soon use to explore the Universe.

It's just possible that Albert did have some genius-type ideas when he was very young, but, if he did, no one remembers them so we'll never know what they were.

1 It's one of the things Albert helped to invent (see page 152).

Hermann and Pauline were nice, easy-going people on the whole. They were Jewish but didn't take Jewish customs too seriously. Hermann in particular was very relaxed, even later on when Albert did strange things like refusing to be German, arranging his own expulsion from school and becoming the greatest scientist ever. Hermann liked nothing better than reading poetry, going for country walks, and good food and drink, while Pauline was really into music, especially the violin (which Albert became very keen on too – and stayed that way for the rest of his life).

In some ways, maybe Hermann was a bit *too* relaxed – he was interested in science and set up several different electrical companies using money borrowed from rich relatives, perhaps without thinking through his plans carefully enough first. To begin with, these companies went quite well and everyone was happy, but then somehow or other they all went bankrupt and Albert's relatives shook their heads and tutted. Especially the ones who'd lent the money.

But this wasn't all his fault. Germany at the time was a tough place to live in...

Hard times

Top-Bit-of-Middle-Part-of-Europe Times

1871

NEW COUNTRY, TO BE CALLED GERMANY, FORMED FROM OVER THREE HUNDRED LITTLE BITS!

MAP-MAKERS' STREET PARTIES DISRUPT TRAFFIC.

Germany was becoming more and more warlike. All men had to do two years of military service, money was poured into making weapons, politicians and even taxi-drivers wore military uniforms, and laws were passed to stop people complaining about it all.

But Albert didn't like military things – when he and Hermann saw some soldiers marching by, Albert said…

But throughout his life he was going to have to deal with all sorts of military people and places, starting off with school. Yes, school. And you thought yours was bad.

Not that Albert was all that peaceful himself at the time – he had a terrible temper, and when he got really angry his nose went white. When he was about five his parents found him a nice teacher, but even at such a tender age Albert made his feelings very clear...

His poor teacher had to go, even though it wasn't her fault. The problem was, Albert didn't like other people telling him things and expecting him just to take their word for it. He liked to work things out for himself. It's just as well really, because he'd never have become dead famous otherwise.

Schools for soldiers

Albert's first school was called Peter's School, and he was nine when he went there. It had over two thousand pupils, seventy in Albert's class. Their lessons consisted of being taught to repeat things over and over again until everyone knew them by heart, and they were encouraged by being hit on the knuckles with a cane.

The teachers tried to make it as much like a little army barracks as possible, and Albert hated it. He was obedient, he didn't make a fuss and he got good marks in most things, but he wasn't happy. He soon became a bit of a loner – as he was to remain for the rest of his life.

After a few years at his first school, he moved on to another, called Luitpold. He hated that one too.

LUITPOLD SCHOOL RULES

1. Latin and Greek are compulsory.
2. Liking Latin and Greek is compulsory.
3. All pupils will learn things by heart. Understanding them doesn't matter.
4. No physics until year seven.
5. No thinking for yourself.
6. No smiling in a superior way.
7. No whingeing about the school rules.

Poor Albert. He didn't like Latin or Greek. What he really liked was physics – did he really have to wait another seven years before he learned any? He'd never become a dead famous physicist at that rate. His teachers certainly didn't think much of his chances. When Hermann asked Albert's teacher what career his son should choose, the teacher said...

Being Jewish was to cause Albert plenty of problems later on in his life, but it was a big help to him just then, because Jewish families have a nice friendly tradition that they should invite a poor Jewish scholar to dinner every week. Hermann and Pauline didn't take Jewish traditions too seriously, but they were nice friendly people so they did invite a medical student called Max Talmud round on

Thursdays. He was twenty-one when he first met Albert (who was ten at the time) and he soon found that Albert liked science and started to lend him all sorts of books about it. Albert loved them and discussed them with Max, who gave Albert more and more difficult ones about the most complicated bits of philosophy as well as science, with all sorts of tempting titles:

ALBERT'S LOST NOTEBOOK

Reading list:

KANT: CRITIQUE OF PURE REASON (A bit too easy).

TEXTBOOK OF PLANE GEOMETRY (Just SO cool. Definitely my favourite).

DARWIN (OK, but I don't really like biology).

But however tricky the books were, Albert understood them all – in fact, he was soon baffling Max with his questions.

But if religion helped Albert to get into science, science got Albert out of religion. When he was about eleven, he became religious in a big way. He'd pray, preach, and read religious books. He even wrote hymns and sang them on the way to school. He read religious books just as he read scientific ones – to learn things. And as usual, he didn't take what he read on trust – it all had to make sense. But the trouble was, the more he read and the more he thought, the less sense it made. Until, one day…

The only thing Albert would ever really trust from now on was science – and then only if he worked through the arguments for himself. But when he started to think about the science he'd learnt, he realized that some of it didn't make any more sense than religion did. These experiences put Albert off school even more – he was expected just to accept everything he was told there, and not to question anything. Albert didn't like that idea at all: he wanted to escape. As soon as possible.

A new life

While Albert wanted to leave but couldn't, Hermann didn't want to leave, but had to. The electrical company he was running with his brother Jakob was in trouble – it was just too small to compete with its increasingly powerful rivals. In 1894, when Albert was 15, it went bankrupt and the family, including Uncle Jakob, moved to Italy. Most of the family, that is…

Hermann and Pauline decided to leave Albert with some distant relations for the time being because they didn't want to interrupt his schooling – his exams were coming up soon. But an interruption to his schooling was just what Albert wanted. Anyway, that was it. He had had enough. There was *no way* he was staying at that school any longer, or with his relations either. Soon he had a cunning plan ready.

So Albert left. It meant he didn't get a diploma, but it also meant he didn't have to do military service. He followed his family to Italy, without telling them he was on his way. They were surprised to see him, but they didn't make a fuss. They didn't even mind too much about his next plan: it wasn't only German schools he was sick of – he didn't like anything about being German. So he decided to stop. He got Hermann to write a letter to renounce his nationality. That didn't mean he was Italian – he wasn't a member of any country any more, and that suited him just fine, because he wasn't interested in nationalities.

Now that Albert had escaped from his horrible German school, he was having fun. He liked Italy a lot, and he also helped out in his Uncle Jakob's factory, where he turned out to be startlingly brainy. No surprise to us of course, but Uncle Jakob was dead impressed, and said: 'Where I and my assistant engineer have racked our brains for days, this young fellow comes along and solves the whole business in a mere quarter-hour. He'll go far one day.' Unfortunately, we don't know what this 'business' was...

Albert's next plan was to find out how the Universe worked. He thought being a science teacher would be a good scheme to earn money while he was doing it – though Hermann was keener on him becoming an electrical engineer. Anyway, for now Albert just wanted to learn more about science, and he knew that the best place to go was the Swiss Polytechnic (which most people called the Poly) in Zurich.

It sounded a great place to Albert:

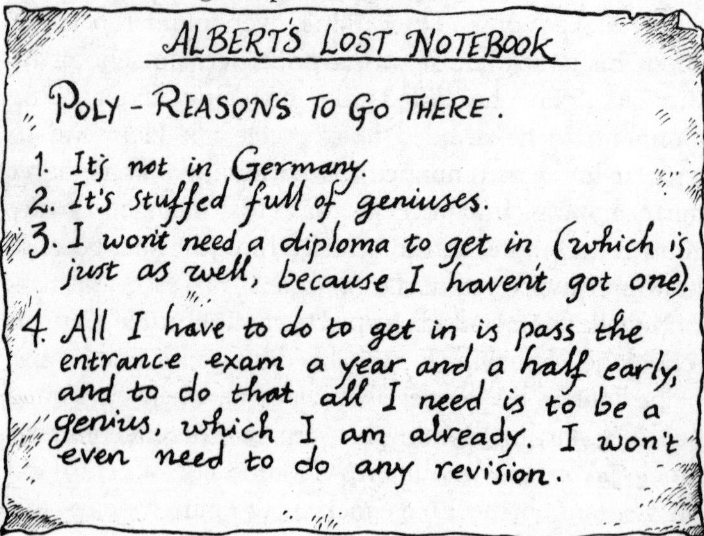

But, sadly:

Actually, Albert didn't have to wait much longer before getting to work on the Universe: it was after only a few months in Aarau, at the age of sixteen, that he asked himself the question that was to take him ten years to answer and which would help him sort out huge chunks of the Universe, solve the mysteries of space and time and make him dead famous:

ABSOLUTELY... NOT?

By the time Albert started to wonder about what travelling at the speed of light would be like, most scientists thought they had explained more or less everything about how the Universe worked: all they needed to do was polish their theories a bit here and there, twiddle with their equations, do a few more experiments and science would be finished and they could all go home.

People like Isaac Newton and his friends (as well as his enemies – he had plenty of those[1]) had come up with mathematical laws that explained all sorts of things, like why the planets move as they do, what causes the tides and why it's so nippy in winter. They had come up with a nice picture of the Universe, full of lumps of this and that which were all made of little hard round atoms that were pushed around by forces of one sort or another. It was all a little bit like a really big game of snooker, but more exciting.

1 See *Dead Famous – Isaac Newton and his Apple*.

Brain Box

Isaac Newton

Isaac Newton will crop up a lot in Albert's story, because in a way they both had the same job – finding mathematical theories to explain how the Universe worked. Until Albert came along, Isaac's theories were the best there were. His main discoveries were:

- How objects move when you push them.
- How to do calculations that no one else could, by inventing a new sort of maths.
- Something about how light works.
- How every bit of matter[1] attracts every other bit of matter through the force of gravity.

But Isaac could never really discover what gravity actually was. Which was very irritating.

Scientists like Isaac could even predict the future, and say where each planet would be next week or next century. There was a lot of fiddly maths to be done, of course, which they had to do themselves because no one had got around to inventing proper computers yet, but any such problem could be solved given time. There were a few oddities like the planet Mercury, which didn't

1 Matter is the thing that everything is made of: it can be in the form of solid, liquid, gas, or weird stuff called plasma.

move quite as they expected – but it's very small and a long way away so no one cared about it much.

Isaac had thought that all the planets and stars and apples and bits of stick and everything were like the pieces of an enormous clockwork machine, built by a God who had set it all going so the planets went round the Sun and the atoms rushed about banging into each other. It all happened in a big featureless nothingy sort of space that went on for ever in all directions, in which time ticked smoothly on – also for ever. It was called absolute space. Some things – like the Sun or people – moved about in this space, and other things didn't. The things that were moving were said to have 'absolute motion' and the things that weren't were said to be 'absolutely at rest'.

What this means sounds obvious – but is it really? If you're reading this book slumped on a sofa with the TV on and a nice cup of tea next to you, you may think *you're* absolutely at rest. But really you're whizzing through space at hundreds of kilometres per hour with the turning Earth. Even if you were at the North Pole (which is like being at the hub of a turning wheel) you wouldn't be absolutely at rest because the Earth is going round the Sun. So what about the Sun? Apart from being a bit on the hot side, it's moving too, on its way round the Galaxy, so you couldn't find absolute rest there either. And, speaking of the Galaxy… Well, you get the idea. Being absolutely at rest isn't as easy as it seems.

This sort of thing didn't worry most scientists when Albert was a nipper – basically they reckoned the Universe was a complicated place full of all sorts of weird things, but that they knew more or less how it all worked. No wonder they felt a bit smug about it. Just so long as no one asked any tricky questions, like:

Questions like this were just unanswerable – or so everyone thought. One day Albert would answer them himself, but for now he was having enough trouble with his own tricky question: what would it be like to travel at the speed of light?

This was one of the questions that led Albert to the Special Theory of Relativity, which was the thing that started to make him dead famous. Relativity explains how the world really is – but it often sounds very strange, and people sometimes say…

But what *is* common sense? It's our feeling of how the world 'should' be, and it's based on our experience of the things we see and do every day: looking at our watches, travelling in cars, going for walks in the country. It's not based on experiences like looking at atomic clocks, travelling about in futuristic spacecraft at thousands of kilometres a second or going for walks on stars as big as a thousand suns. If we did these things, we'd all be as good at relativity as Albert, because relativity would be just common sense to us.

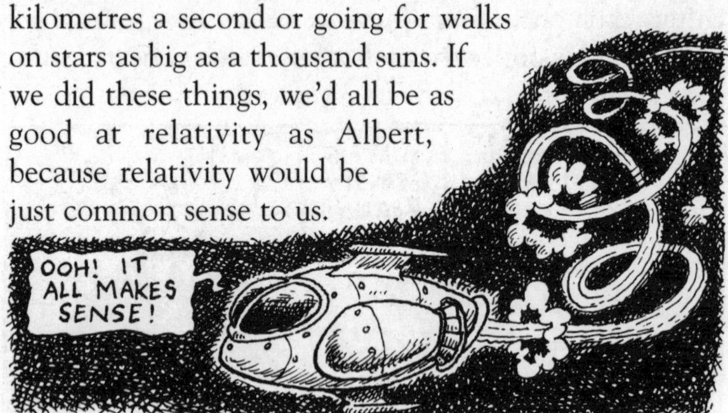

Anyway, we know common sense is often wrong – isn't it just common sense that the Earth is flat?

Brain Box

Relativity

Maybe this is a good time to let you in on a little secret. Albert's theory of relativity, which revolutionized physics, is all about one really really basic idea. It's very simple, but it's also a bit stunning, though it may not sound like it at first. The idea is…

THERE IS NO SUCH THING AS ABSOLUTE MOTION.

The only sort of motion that exists is RELATIVE motion (which is why it's called Relativity). It's worth droning on about this point a bit, because it will make everything else a lot clearer.

Imagine that in the whole Universe there is only a planet and a sun. No other planets, no moons, no stars. You are standing on the planet and you can see the sun slowly moving across the sky. Why does it do that?

Is it possible to show who is right?

No. You can assume either that the planet is spinning or that the sun is going round it (or both) and no one could prove you were wrong. In fact, it doesn't even mean anything to ask the question – it's a bit like saying: 'Am I taller than you, or are you shorter than me?' This is a tricky idea to get hold of – that though you could choose to say the sun was really moving and the planet wasn't, that's all it would be – just a choice, not a fact. The only fact is that the sun changes its position in the sky, showing that it is moving *relative* to you.

What Albert was able to prove is that this relative motion is the only sort there is. It's quite possible to *assume* that the Earth is still and the Moon and the Sun and all the stars and galaxies move around it in complicated paths, but again, it's a choice, not a fact or a false statement. It's a choice most of us make most of the time. But the Apollo astronauts treated the Earth as if it was moving when they were on the Moon. Then, they assumed the Moon was still. People make whatever choice makes it simpler to talk about things.

When you say 'The car is moving at ten metres per second,' people know you mean 'The car is moving at ten metres per second compared to (relative to) the ground.' But you *could* say, 'The car is moving at thirty thousand metres per second compared to the Sun,' or, 'The car is moving at 250 thousand metres per second compared to the centre of the Galaxy.' Or, 'The car isn't moving at all compared to the fluffy dice.'

All these statements are true. Which one you say is just a matter of choice. What you can't do is to say how fast the car is 'really' moving, without reference to anything else at all.

By the time Albert came along, scientists thought they'd discovered a way to find out about the absolute motion of objects. They decided there was an absolutely still invisible something called the 'ether' which filled the whole of space. The absolute speed of the Earth would be its speed through the ether, so all they had to do was measure this speed. Sadly, they found they couldn't, and were all most upset until Albert sorted it out for them.

There's been a lot of argy-bargy ever since about whether the failed experiments to study the ether were the starting-point for Albert's theory of relativity. Even Albert seemed unsure, but on the whole he said that they weren't, and his actual papers and arguments hardly mention the ether – one of them just points out in passing that there's no need to believe in it any more[1]. Thanks to Albert, no one needed to worry about measuring absolute motion any more, because he'd shown there was no such thing.

No one is saying there is no such thing as motion, just that the only sort of motion that exists is relative motion. It's the only sort that actually means anything. Not a very interesting thing to say? Just wait and see what Albert does with it…

1 We'll come across the ether again on page 147.

SCARY SCIENCE WARNING

Some of this next bit might seem a bit tricky at first, but there's no maths and a summary on page 45.

In the world of relativity, the best way to measure speeds isn't in kilometres per second or miles per hour, but as a fraction of the speed of light: so instead of going at 150 thousand kilometres per second, you'd say you were going at half the speed of light, or 0.5 times *c*, or just 0.5*c* (the speed of light is often written as 'c'). It's only when things go at a reasonable fraction of the speed of light that relativity really starts to make itself noticed.

Light goes really fast. Really *really* fast. Maybe it takes you ten minutes to walk to the shops? Light could have gone there and back ten million times by the time you get your shoes on. If it felt like it, light could go seven times round the Earth in a second, or nip across to the Moon in under two.

But imagine you were used to these sort of speeds, and you could move millions of times faster than normal – so going at half the speed of light would be a gentle stroll for you rather than a mind-boggling, breath-taking, stomach-churning ZZZZZZZZZZOOM. (Or you can imagine that light travels incredibly slowly – a few metres a second – if you like, rather than that you go incredibly fast.) What, Albert wondered, would happen?

He was sure that that sort of carry-on would have a hair-raising effect on the Principle of Relativity

No, he invented the *Theory* of Relativity, not the *Principle* of Relativity. The Principle of Relativity had been knocking about for centuries, and one way of saying it is: 'The laws of nature are the same whether you're standing still or moving steadily along in a straight line'.

It is. The world would be a weird place if the Principle of Relativity was wrong – imagine what would happen if your watch went backwards when you were on a skateboard, or if people turned inside-out on trains.

So: if you're standing on a moving train and drop a Walkman it will smash at your feet, just the same as if you're standing on the ground: the Principle of Relativity means that Newton's laws work just the same as usual. BUT if the train is braking or lurching or going round a bend, the Principle doesn't apply – the

Walkman will smash somewhere else. If the train is braking really hard, the Walkman might even smash into the wall in front of you. For the next few chapters, we're talking about really well-behaved trains that go absolutely straight, with no wobbling about and no changing speed. Let's call this 'smooth' motion to keep things short.

The Principle of Relativity sounds a bit boring, like when someone says, 'If you eat all that chocolate you'll feel sick.' It's so obvious, it's irritating. But when Albert started to work out what the Principle really meant it was to lead him to some amazing conclusions about time.

The mystery of motion

The Principle can be worded in a different way – if the laws of nature aren't affected by motion, that means no experiment or machine or measurement or observation will be affected either; in other words, there's no way to tell you're moving or not. So...

THE PRINCIPLE OF RELATIVITY

THERE IS NO MEASUREMENT YOU CAN MAKE THAT WILL TELL YOU WHETHER YOU'RE STATIONARY OR MOVING SMOOTHLY.

This sounds a bit strange – everyone knows when they're moving, don't they? Or do they?

If you were in a train, how could you convince an argumentative friend that it was moving?

Dropping a Walkman doesn't do any good either, especially not to the Walkman, and it's the same with any other experiment you try: there's no way you can tell the difference between smooth motion and stillness.

Do they? People know trains and things are moving *relative* to the Earth – but can you think of a way to *prove* that it's the train that's really moving, rather than the Earth? This is the same problem that cropped up on page 24 – how do you know whether you're absolutely at rest or not?

This is so important to Albert's theory, we'll say it again: 'There is no measurement you can make that will tell you whether you're stationary or moving smoothly.'

Albert was fascinated by this idea, and he wanted to explore it further. Was it really true, *however* fast things went? No one had ever found anything that could go faster than light, and this is why Albert imagined himself travelling at this mega speed: 300 million metres per second. As far as anyone knew there was nothing very special about this speed, other than that light happened to travel that fast – just like there's nothing very special about 330 metres per second, except that it happens to be the speed of sound.

Having imagined himself going at the speed of light, Albert knew just what he'd do next...

But we don't. No one knows quite what went through Albert's amazing brain to get him from his idea about travelling at the speed of light to his stunning conclusions about time, but the next chapter explains one way of getting there...

ALBERT CONQUERS TIME

SCARY SCIENCE WARNING

This section could make you feel a bit...

...but there are no equations and, when you've read it, you'll have found a way to slow down time.

Let's try Albert's approach of investigating whether common-sense ideas of speed, light and time still make sense, however fast you go. Imagine you're in a train, which is miraculously travelling at the speed of light. You'll be on the planet Mars in a few minutes (so I hope you weren't planning to visit your Auntie Ethel in Brighton), but you've got time to have a little look at the back wall of the carriage first.

Spookily enough, you can't see it. In fact, you can't see anything in that direction at all. Why not? Because you can only see something if light rays can travel from the thing to your eyes. The light-rays from the back of the carriage must be travelling at the speed of light (as you'd expect of any self-respecting light-ray), but you're travelling at the speed of light too, so the rays from the back of the carriage will never reach you. So there's nothing to see!

Weird. And worse: remember the Principle of Relativity? 'There is no measurement you can make that will tell you whether you're stationary or moving smoothly.'

But you've just found what seems to be a foolproof test which could tell you you *are* moving: if you can't see the back wall of the carriage, then you must be moving (at the speed of light). But the Principle of Relativity says there is *no* test that can show this.

Baffling, or what? The Principle of Relativity is a really basic law. Surely it can't possibly be wrong?

Let's assume it's right and see what happens. That means you can't use the way the carriage looks to tell you you're moving. So it must look normal to you, however fast it's going. The only way it can look normal is if the light from the back of the carriage reaches your eyes as it normally would.

There's no other answer – if the Principle of Relativity

is right, then the carriage must look normal to you and the light must behave in its normal way. It can only do this if the light ignores the motion of the train entirely, and travels at its usual speed from the carriage walls to your eyes – just as if the train isn't moving at all. The speed of light would have to be the same for everyone, whether they were moving or not.

This might not sound strange, but it is. Incredibly strange. Albert realized that it means that light behaves quite differently from other moving things. A cricketer bowls a ball while he or she is running, because the ball ends up going faster than if it were thrown from a standstill. The ball is already moving with the bowler at whatever speed they can run, and is pushed to a higher speed when it is bowled.

If it weren't for Albert, one would expect that if a bowler shone a torch instead of throwing a ball the result would be a light-beam that travelled at the normal speed of light *plus* the speed of the bowler's run. But Albert's theory means that this isn't true, and that however fast the bowler runs the light will shine at the same old speed of 300 million metres per second. Even if the bowler runs towards the batsman at the speed of light and shines the torch ahead, and if the batsman measures the speed of the torchlight, the answer will still be only 300 million metres per second.

Despite the weirdness of this conclusion, Albert decided to have a go at assuming it was really true – that light travelled at the same speed for everyone – and see where that took him. This is another of those really important things, so...

THE SPEED OF LIGHT IS THE SAME FOR EVERYONE, NO MATTER HOW FAST THEY'RE GOING.

This odd fact, which has been proved right loads of times, only affects light (and other similar things like radio-waves that go at the same speed). It isn't true of sound, for instance: if you run away from a sound wave, you'll measure its speed as slower than if you stand still. Go fast enough, and you can escape from sound – just as people in supersonic planes do. They can't hear the roar of the engines because they are moving faster than the sound is. But you can never escape from a light ray – however fast you run, it will always shine on you, and it will always be travelling at the same speed when it does.

But why? How could Albert explain this strange fact? He asked himself: what is speed really? It's just a measure of the *time* taken to travel a certain distance.

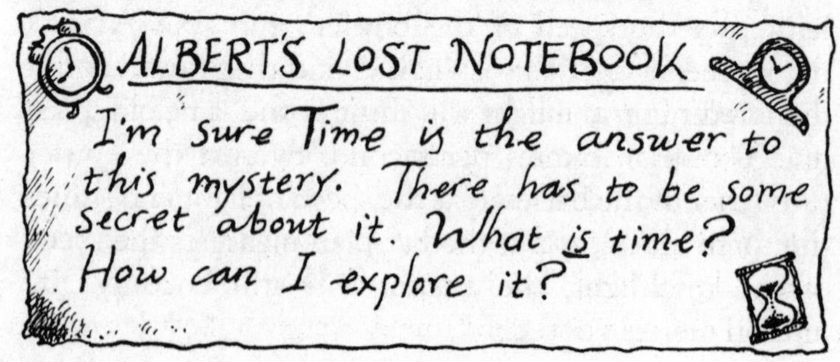

One way to explore time is with a clock. A clock like...

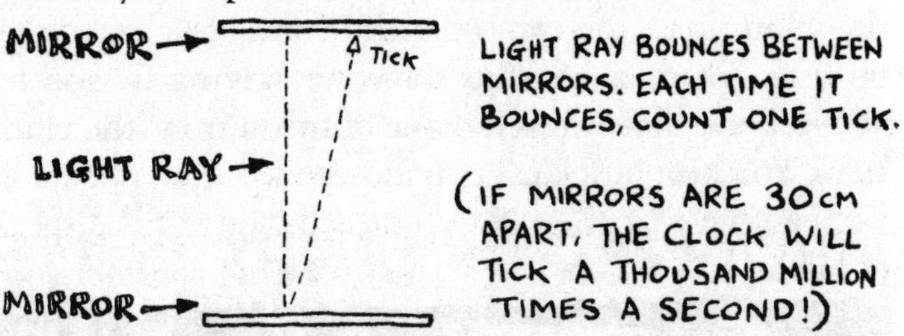

This sort of clock isn't brilliant, because – a) it's only imaginary, and b) to use it to boil an egg you'd have to count up to two hundred thousand million.

But a light-clock is a nice simple thing to think about (much simpler than a lot of cogs and a cuckoo) and we already know that thinking about light is a good way of exploring the effects of high-speed travel. So imagine sending your light-clock on a high-speed journey. What would happen as it moved faster and faster?

Well, imagine again that you're used to moving around at hundreds of millions of metres a second, so light seems to move quite slowly to you, and a hundredth of a millionth of a second (which is ten nanoseconds) seems a reasonably long time.

A friend called Gerald stands in front of you, holding the light clock, and you concentrate on the light ray – which looks like a bright point of light to you – moving up and down in a straight line inside the clock. It's night, and you can only see your friend and the clock vaguely – the main thing you can see is the point of light moving up and down, a bit like someone waving a sparkler about. Each time it reaches one of the mirrors, the clock ticks. You hear a tick every nanosecond. And, of course, you can see that the light point is moving at the speed of light.

Don't fall asleep – something weird is about to happen any nanosecond now...

Now, Gerald starts walking at about a quarter the speed of light, carrying the ticking light clock. What do you see the point of light doing now?

Now Gerald starts to run. The zigzag now looks like this:

This is the point: the faster Gerald goes past you, the further that point of light has to go to get to the bottom of the light clock. (Just measure one of the zigs in the last picture – it's longer than a zig in the picture before, and longer still than when Gerald isn't moving at all.)

Oh no it doesn't. It *can't* go faster. Remember: The speed of light is the same for everyone, no matter how fast they're going.

So, if it has to go farther and it can't speed up, that means it must take *longer* to reach the bottom of the clock and make a tick. So there is a longer time between ticks. So, in other words, *the clock slows down*.

By the way, before we explore the mysteries of time, space and going really really fast any further, there are three things to bear in mind:

1 As far as Gerald is concerned, the light isn't zigzagging. He's carrying the clock with him, so he still sees the light bouncing up and down, same old distance, same old speed, same old time between ticks.

2 This is weirdly different to what happens to things which move at everyday speeds: imagine Gerald standing in front of you playing with a yo-yo. It will move up and down at a certain speed – maybe it takes a second to go up and down once. Now, if Gerald runs past you, the yo-yo will make a zigzag path like the picture on page 40 (or the last picture if he's really nippy). But all this means is that the yo-yo goes along with Gerald at whatever speed he's running, as well as going up and down at the same old speed. It still takes a second to go up and down. This means its total speed is higher than if Gerald was standing still. There's no problem with this, because there's no law which says: "The speed of a yo-yo is the same for everyone, no matter how fast they're going."

3 Things do have to rush about a bit before these effects become noticeable: if you sent your second-favourite watch on a 75 kilometre-per-second journey for a whole year, it would still end up being only one second slower than the watch on your wrist. But if the effects were obvious, we wouldn't have needed Albert to work them out...

If moving light-clocks run slow, what about other things? The Principle of Relativity says there's no test that someone in a moving vehicle can do to find out they are moving. But the light-clock slows down at high speeds – won't this slowing down show people on board that they are moving? Not if the people slow down too! Therefore: everything in the vehicle must slow down – all types of clock, all machines, and even the bodies and thoughts of travellers. TIME ITSELF MUST SLOW DOWN IN A MOVING VEHICLE. Only then will no one on board notice that the clock is slowing down and only in that way can the Principle of Relativity still be true. No one on board will notice any changes at all, because everything they look at inside the vehicle will be affected as they are. Only to someone outside the vehicle will the slowing-down of time on board be visible.

SECRETS OF SPACE AND TIME
Number One:
TIME SLOWS DOWN IN A MOVING VEHICLE.

So if you put your Auntie Ethel in a see-through rocket and accelerated it to near the speed of light while you stayed safely on the ground, you would see the movements of her body and the flashing of her light-clock get slower and slower as the vehicle got faster and faster. It's impossible for Ethel to travel at the speed of light but she could get very, very close to light speed, and then her movements would be almost completely frozen.

Auntie Ethel, looking back at you through her handy telescope, would see just the same sort of strange things happening. While her light-clock and her heart and mind went on ticking and pulsing and thinking at their usual rates, she would see everything outside slowing down. As the speed of light was approached, birds would hover in the air hardly flapping their wings, rivers would move as slowly as snails and you would look like a living statue.

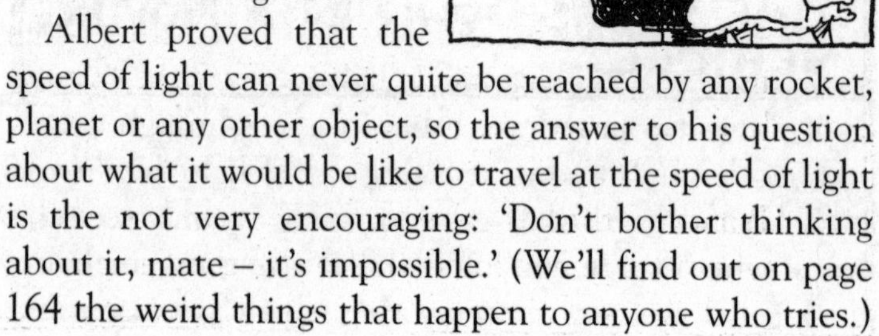

Albert proved that the speed of light can never quite be reached by any rocket, planet or any other object, so the answer to his question about what it would be like to travel at the speed of light is the not very encouraging: 'Don't bother thinking about it, mate – it's impossible.' (We'll find out on page 164 the weird things that happen to anyone who tries.)

But asking the question did lead to some amazing answers, including the slowing down of time at very high speeds.

And that is the key to the Special Theory of Relativity. Here's a summary

NEW! FUN-SIZE

EINSTEIN'S EINCREDIBLE THEORIES: TIME AND MOTION

1 The laws of nature are the same whether you're moving or not (The Principle of Relativity).

2 This means you can't tell for sure whether you're moving or not.

3 But you might expect there would be one way to tell whether you're moving: if you move at the speed of light, you'd think the inside of your vehicle would look different (because rays from the back could never catch up with you).

4 But we don't want to accept that the Principle of Relativity could be wrong. The only alternative is to say the speed of light is the same whether you're moving or not. Then the inside of your vehicle will always look the same, however fast you're going.

5 But even then there seems to be a way to tell when you're moving and disprove the Principle

of Relativity: if you carry a light-clock it would tick more slowly (because the light would have further to go between ticks to keep up with the moving mirrors).

6 The only way round this one is if EVERYTHING in the moving vehicle – even your mind – slows down with the light clock.

7 This means *time slows down in a moving vehicle* – as seen by someone outside it.

8 Although the travellers in the vehicle wouldn't see anything odd going on inside, they'd see things happening outside slowing down.

And, by the way, if all this just seems like a clever argument, hang on until page 66 – where we'll see some evidence that the Universe really is like this.

But Albert's discoveries about time were just the start.

ALBERT ESCAPES

It took a long time – about ten years – for Albert to discover the secret of time, and to sort out the sums that would allow him to work out exactly how time changes at different speeds. One reason it took that long is that it was all so amazingly weird, but another was that Albert was busy with other things during those ten years.

The teachers at Aarau weren't wildly impressed with Albert:

The High School, Aarau, Switzerland
Report on Albert Einstein, Age 16

Physics.	More work needed.
Chemistry	Poor.
Italian.	Bad.
French.	Terrible
Singing.	Just don't ask!
P.E.	DON'T EVEN THINK ABOUT IT!

But never mind, Albert had fun there and, anyway, he soon improved. It was a real new start for him – he had stopped being German, stopped being religious, moved schools and even had a new family to live with, the Wintelers. He got on so well with them that he fell in love with the daughter, Marie, who was eighteen (this was when Albert was sixteen). It was fun while it lasted, but that wasn't very long – we don't know why but Albert broke it off after a few months.

It was soon time for Albert to do some more exams. He did fairly well – well enough to get him into the Poly anyway. He had a lot of fun there too, but the only things he took seriously were some of the science lectures.

Albert talked a lot about science with all his friends, but with Friedrich Adler there were also lots of conversations about politics. Friedrich was very left-wing, and Albert agreed with him – though at that stage he didn't take it too seriously. He certainly wouldn't have – oh, I don't know – assassinated anyone for political reasons. But then, who would?

Meanwhile, Albert was being a bit of a disappointment to his teachers. He didn't like many of his lessons, and he *hated* exams.

Albert was actually very keen on physics – but he preferred to be his own teacher. He read every book about it he could get his hands on. He especially liked electromagnetism, and James Clerk Maxwell was one of his heroes. James had collected together every fact that was known about electricity and magnetism, and come up with four fairly simple equations that included all of them. Reducing a huge complicated part of the world to a few equations was what Isaac Newton had done for motion and gravity, and it was just the sort of thing that Albert was determined to do for the whole Universe.

Problems

In 1900 Albert reluctantly took his final exams and did reasonably well. He decided to settle down, get a nice job, marry Mileva, and solve the mysteries of the Universe. But...

YOU'LL NEVER MARRY MILEVA! SHE'S COMMON, POOR AND UNHEALTHY. SHE'D JUST BE A BURDEN TO YOU!
SPORT
SO CAN I HAVE A JOB AT THE POLY THEN, HERR PERNET?
NO. YOU'RE TOO ARROGANT, AND YOUR EXAM RESULTS WEREN'T GOOD ENOUGH.
OOH! WHAT'S THIS?
ZURICH DISTRICT COUNCIL
MEDICAL REVIEW BOARD
13 March 1901
Dear Mr Einstein,
Thank you for attending the medical examination last week. We regret to inform you that the examining doctor reports that you are unfit for Swiss military service due to your flat feet and varicose veins.
Yours sincerely

Hermann even wrote to a famous chemist called Wilhelm Ostwald, asking for a job for Albert, but it was no good. Finally Albert managed to get a temporary job as a teacher in a technical college – the only problem was that the subject was descriptive geometry, which Albert had skived off at Poly. After this he got another teaching job, as a private tutor this time. He had to live and eat with his employer to start with, but he didn't like that at all. So he started so many arguments he was allowed to live in a hotel and eat in a restaurant instead – at his employer's expense.

Luckily, Albert's friend Marcel worked at the Swiss Patent Office and had heard of a vacancy there, so Albert moved to Bern, where the Office was. While he was waiting for the job to be officially advertised, Albert, who was now very poor, put an advert in the paper. Maybe it looked a bit like this...

FREE LESSONS IN MATHS OR PHYSICS

For a limited period only, a soon-to-be-world-famous[1] genius is offering, EXCLUSIVELY TO READERS OF THIS ADVERT, a FREE private lesson in Maths or Physics. Later lessons may be purchased for a small[2] fee.

MONEY BACK IF NOT DELIGHTED[3]

FREE LIGHT CLOCK[4] FOR FIRST APPLICANT

NO SALESMAN WILL CALL

To take advantage of this EXCLUSIVE FREE offer, contact:

ALBERT EINSTEIN, 32 Justice Lane, Bern.

Ask about our very reasonably priced mystery-solving[5] service.

1 Honest.
2 Relatively.
3 On first lesson ONLY.
4. Latest imaginary model.
5. Mysteries of the Universe only.

A Romanian student called Maurice Solovine answered the advert, and he and Albert got on very well, and discussed all sorts of other things after the official lessons had ended. They were soon joined by Conrad Habicht, who was studying to be a maths teacher, and the three of them had such fun discussing science, philosophy and things that they decided to invent a special society to do it in:

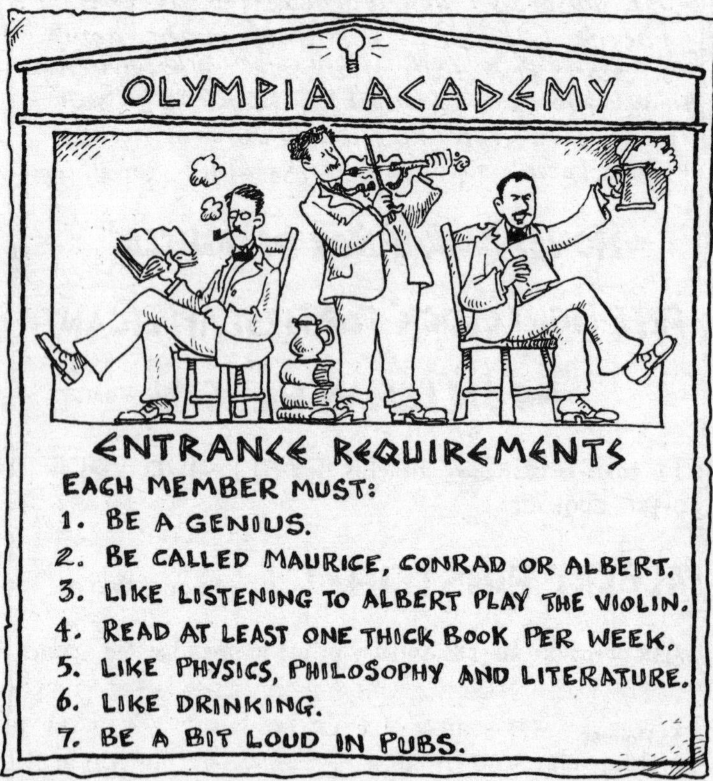

So that kept Albert busy when he wasn't sorting out the Universe or looking for a job. Finally, the advert for the Patent Office job appeared and he applied – and got it.

It was a nice job for Albert – people would design wonderful inventions and he'd work out the essentials and see whether they made sense. Sussing out the basic principles was exactly the treatment he was giving to the Universe just then.

ALBERT'S LOST NOTEBOOK

At last I've got a great job in the Patent Office – it's only eight hours a day, six days a week. I'm giving one or two private lessons per day too, as well as going to the Olympia Society meetings and doing the reading for them. So that leaves me plenty of time for discovering the meaning of the Universe (I'm working on time, light particles, atoms and statistics at the moment). So the only question is – what shall I do in my spare time?

PATENT APPLICATION

But it wasn't all fun for Albert. Mileva, who was living miles away in Hungary with her parents, was pregnant and their daughter Lieserl was born there in 1902, while Albert was in Bern. Albert kept this secret, maybe because he was scared of what his family might do, or maybe because he thought he would lose his job at the Patent Office if he were known to have had a child without being married. In those days, the idea of children born outside of marriage like this was so shocking for a lot of people that they'd do almost anything to keep it quiet.

Hermann and Pauline – especially Pauline – had never liked Mileva (no one really knows why), and they refused to give their permission for a marriage. Although this wasn't legally required, Albert didn't want to marry without it. Hermann did give in in the end, but only when he was dying. Only the Olympia Academy attended the wedding.

Lieserl was left with Mileva's parents for a while and was probably then adopted by someone – no one knows who. Albert never saw his daughter and never mentioned her again as far as anyone knows. The year after the marriage, Albert and Mileva's first son, Hans Albert, was born.

Despite all this, Albert kept working at his amazing theories until, in 1905, he was ready to tell everyone about them. In Albert's day – and today too – the main way that scientists published their results was in the form of technical articles called papers. That year, Albert published four, plus a very nice PhD thesis. One paper was about the theory he'd been working on for ten years: relativity.

STRETCHED TIME, SQUASHED SPACE

Albert had worked out that moving clocks must run slow if the Principle of Relativity is true. This was to become one of the most important bits of his Special Theory of Relativity. But before he could go any further, Albert needed to do some maths to work out just *how* slow clocks go at very high speeds.

(NOT SO) SCARY SCIENCE WARNING

You might assume this sort of maths would look all $\frac{x^2}{12.546b^3} - \Upsilon^{99} + \exp[y^3-42]$ ish, and that only geniuses can understand it. Well, although it's not *dead* easy, it's much simpler than, say, GCSE maths or tap dancing.

Remember Gerald running past with the light-clock? Let's say the light-clock is a metre long. And let's also say he's going half as fast as the light (which, as we know, goes at about 300 million metres per second, so he's running at about 150 million metres per second).

OK, what do we want to do? We want to compare how fast the clock ticks when it's moving past with how fast it ticks when it isn't. Then we'll know exactly how speed affects time.

When the clock isn't moving, the light goes straight down – at the speed of light. The clock is 1 metre long, and light travels 300 million metres every second, so to go one metre, it will only take $\frac{1}{300{,}000{,}000}$ second (which is about 0.0000000033 of a second, or 3.3 nanoseconds). The light-path will look like this:

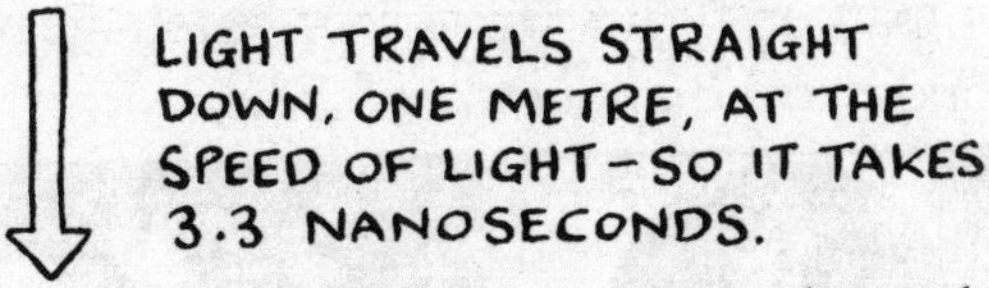

LIGHT TRAVELS STRAIGHT DOWN, ONE METRE, AT THE SPEED OF LIGHT – SO IT TAKES 3.3 NANOSECONDS.

We can use this as one line in a triangle, and we'll be able to measure the length of the longest line of the triangle to find out exactly what speed does to time. The light takes 3.3 nanoseconds to go straight down the light clock, so we'll make our line 3.3 cm long.

When the clock is moving past (being carried by Gerald) at half the speed of light, the light goes along as well as down. Gerald is going half as fast as the light, so his path (the horizontal line) must be half as long as the sloping line the light makes. There is only one triangle we can draw whose sloping line is twice as long as its horizontal line:

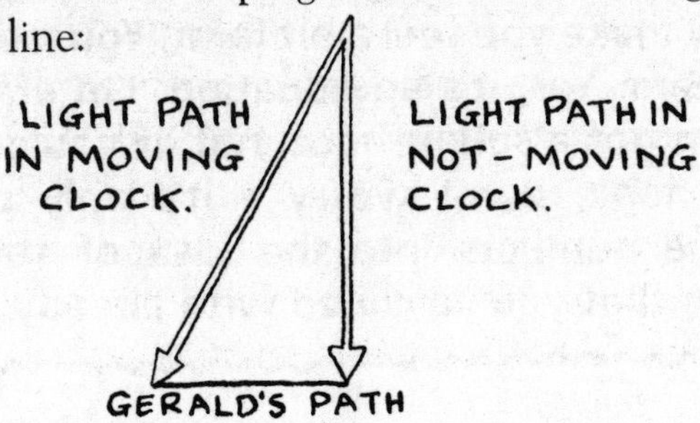

LIGHT PATH IN MOVING CLOCK.

LIGHT PATH IN NOT-MOVING CLOCK.

GERALD'S PATH

The length of the sloping line gives us the time it takes for light to travel down the clock when it's moving past at half the speed of light. If you measure it, you'll find it's 3.8 cm long – so light must take 3.8 nanoseconds to go that far.

So that means, if it takes 3.3 nanoseconds for the clock to tick when it's still, it takes 3.8 nanoseconds to tick when it's moving past you at half the speed of light. So if a rocket moves past you at half the speed of light, you'd be able to see 3.3 nanoseconds (or 3.3 minutes, or 3.3 hours) pass on board, while your watch measures 3.8 nanoseconds (or 3.8 minutes, or 3.8 hours).

DO NOT LOOK AT THE NEXT PAGE IF YOU ARE OF A NERVOUS DISPOSITION

There is something on the next page that may make you feel a bit faint. You may even scream. Yes, it's an equation. I'm afraid it's even got a square root in it. If you'd rather not look, don't worry – it's only putting some numbers into the idea of stretched time that you've coped with already.

Albert didn't need to draw diagrams all over the place to work out the way time stretches. He came up with a nifty little equation (which he got by using Pythagoras' Theorem) which gives the same answer:

By the way: t = amount of time that passes for you, according to a clock you carry; T = amount of time that passes on moving object; s = speed of moving object (in text books, this is 'v' for velocity); and c = speed of light.

We can put numbers in place of the letters to show it works:

You can use this equation to answer tricky questions like…

To make your light-clock more useful, you might add a counter and dial to it so that it was more like an ordinary clock – then you wouldn't haven't to keep counting up to a few billion each time you wanted to use it. You could go into business and sell your clocks all over the Universe! Until Albert came along, scientists thought that time ticked away at the same rate all over the Universe, so your light-clocks would all tell the same time wherever they went and whatever happened to them (so long as no one sat on one). But once Albert found that time flows at different rates depending on how fast you're moving, that meant that different people would see different clocks telling different times. So you can't say 'It's 7 o'clock on Earth and meanwhile it's also 7 o'clock on Alpha Centauri'. In fact, it's never quite safe to use the word 'meanwhile'. You could even say:

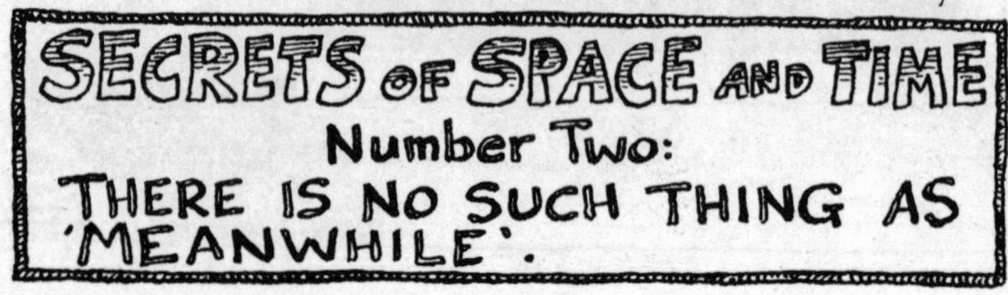

Squashed Space

It wasn't just time that Albert tackled. Space wasn't safe either: he found a way to squash it. To see how, let's talk about trains.

By the way, everyone who likes relativity is obsessed with talking about trains, and if you're ever on a train and someone asks you 'Does Edinburgh stop at this train?', don't worry, they're not mad, they're only a scientist. Unless of course...

Anyway, imagine that Ian, Nicola, Graham and Georgina decide to measure how long a train is. When it's standing quietly in the station they measure it with rulers and find that it is 12 metres long. But what about its length when it's moving at, say, 120 million metres per second? How can they measure that?

Luckily – if a bit mysteriously – they're all armed with little ray-guns. (Nothing deadly though.) Also, they're all wearing accurate watches they have set to the same time at a little meeting they had over lunch. If they time how long it takes a ray to travel along the train, they can work out its length, just by multiplying this time by the speed of the ray (which is the speed of light). So, on board the train, Georgina, who's standing at the front, fires her ray-gun at Nicola, who's at the back:

Georgina notes the time she pulls the trigger. Nicola notes the time when the beam hits her. Then they do a little sum to work out the distance the light has travelled:

Length of train = speed of light × time difference

Let's say the time difference is 0.00000004 second. They work out from this that the train is exactly 12 metres long (because 300,000,000 × 0.00000004 = 12). Just the same length as they found with their rulers when the train was standing in the station. No surprise there then.

So 12 metres is the length according to Georgina and Nicola. What happens when Graham and Ian, outside the moving train, measure the length in the same way?

Graham watches and notes the time when Georgina fires the laser, and Ian notes the time when the laser hits Nicola. They do the same sum – and find the train is only 11 metres long! This is why:

As far as Graham and Ian are concerned, while the light-ray travels down the carriage to hit Nicola, Nicola, with the carriage, has time to move along a bit, to meet the light beam on its way. So for Graham and Ian the train is shorter than for Georgina and Nicola – in other words, if a train is moving past it's shorter than if it isn't. Or...

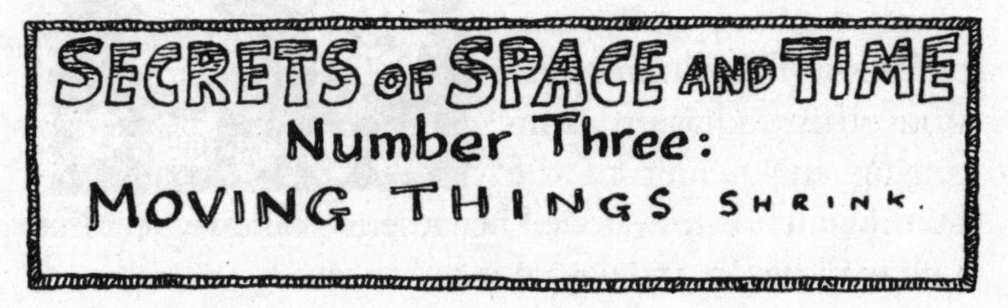

Albert found, when he did the sums, that there was something very familiar about the equation that described how much shorter moving things get:

It really is. For example, there's this little particle called a muon. Muons are very small – much smaller than atoms – and they have short but exciting lives lasting a few millionths of a second, as we know from observing tame ones in laboratories.

Muons are formed high above the Earth, more than ten kilometres above your head, where scary radiation from outer space lurks about. The radiation makes muons by smacking into atoms which drift about up there minding their own business. The atmosphere stops this radiation from getting any nearer to the Earth, which is just as well because it would fry you like a plate of bacon and eggs if it got to you.

Muons come in very handy for proving Albert right. There's something weird about them: there are loads of them crashing into the Earth's surface, but they couldn't have formed nearby, because of the lack of deadly radiation hereabouts.

What's weird about that? Well, let's work out how fast the muons would have to travel to get to the Earth before going PHUT.

They have to travel at least ten kilometres, and they have their whole lives to do it in, which, for some muons (about 1 in 6) is as long as four millionths of a second. How fast would they have to go to make it to the Earth? To go ten kilometres (that's 10,000 metres) in four millionths of a second (that's 0.000004 second), their speed must be 10,000 ÷ 0.000004, or 2,500,000,000 metres per second.

As usual in relativity, it all depends on your point of view. If muons wore little wristwatches, they would show that only about four millionths of a second had passed by the time they'd finished their journey. Yet they last for about forty millionths of a second according to people on the Earth!

The time difference is because the muons are so sporty – they go at very nearly the speed of light. Which just goes to show that Albert was right and time moves slowly when things move fast.

NEW! FUN-SIZE

EINSTEIN'S EINCREDIBLE THEORIES: SPECIAL RELATIVITY

Working from the ideas that there's no measurement you can make that will tell you you're really moving, and that the speed of light is the same for everyone, Albert's massive brain worked out how strange the Universe really is:

1 Because there's no way to tell that something is really moving, all you can really say is that something is moving compared to ('relative' to) something else.

2 According to your watch, time slows down on a vehicle moving past you. (According to someone on the vehicle, it's you whose time slows down.)

3 According to your ruler, a vehicle moving past you squashes. (According to someone on the vehicle, it's you who get squashed.)

4 It's never safe to say that two things in different places happen at the same time.

After all that mind-boggling science, let's see how Albert's getting on at the Patent Office.

ALBERT AND THE SCIENCE-GOD

Once Albert had published his papers, it didn't take long for scientists to notice that there was a genius around – though they were all amazed that he had an ordinary job in the Patent Office. They thought he must at least work in a university (in fact a lot of people sent letters to him at the local one).

Of course, such a stunning new theory as Relativity was bound to upset some of them. A few made silly criticisms that showed they didn't understand what Albert was on about, and others just refused to believe it because it was so weird it got on their nerves.

One person who was a big help to Albert was Max Planck. He turns up again later on, but at the moment what matters is that he was a co-editor of *Annals of Physics*, a kind of magazine for boffins, one of the best there was. Max's job was to decide whether to accept any theoretical papers that were sent in, including Albert's mind-numbingly brilliant ones. Really Max was quite a traditional kind of a physicist who much preferred science to stay just the way it was and not go all strange and modern, but he was also intensely brainy, as well as being a nice bloke, so he was happy not only to accept Albert's paper, but also to tell everyone else how clever Albert was (which was bound to be more effective than Albert doing it himself).

So Albert's amazing paper on how to stretch time and squeeze space was published with no problems at all. There were some unusual things about it:

- It didn't have a list of the other papers it was based on (because it wasn't).
- It included a thank-you note to Michele Besso, his friend at the Patent Office, who had discussed Albert's ideas with him as they walked home from work (very slowly, because Mileva didn't like Michele).

Oh yes, and:

- It was incredibly amazing and changed people's understanding of the Universe for ever.

A lot of the scientists who read Albert's paper didn't understand it, but most of those who did loved it. It was so elegant and explained everything so nicely they felt it just HAD to be true. It was just as well they felt like this, because they had to wait over 25 years for some solid evidence to back it up.

If this sounds a bit odd, that's because experiments didn't matter much to Albert's theories. Almost all the work he did was so advanced that the technology needed to make the measurements to prove it hadn't been invented at the time. For most of his discoveries, mathematics wasn't too important either, except to work out the exact consequences of a theory or prove it to other people. And Albert certainly didn't mind at all if no one else thought he was right about something.

So how did Albert know when he was right about the Universe? Because he believed in God.

Well, sort of (we'll get to that later). But it wasn't a Jewish God Albert used to talk about. Anyway, he'd gone off religion in a big way when he was eleven.

Albert believed in a sort of mathematical scientific kind of God. In fact, the more he discussed it, the less God-like this whatever-it-was sounded. When Albert talked about God, he meant a sort of simplicity in the Universe. For instance, the fact that a simple maths formula like Albert's famous $E = mc^2$ (which we'll get to on page 167) described the Universe was really a surprising thing. After all, why shouldn't it be $E = 0.98mc^{2.00279}$. Or (for that matter):

It's this mysterious underlying *simplicity* that Albert meant when he talked about God. Anyway, that simplicity was what he was looking for, and when he found it, he just knew he was right, whatever other people or experiments might say.

Albert had an incredible year in 1905 – he sorted out atoms, light, time and space (as we'll see in later chapters). When he'd done all that, he stopped for a while – not because he was tired or anything. It's just that he'd run out of things to explain.

Doctor Einstein

Having revolutionized the whole world in about sixteen different ways, Albert had proved he was a really great scientist. Wasn't it about time he became a Doctor of Science? To do that, he had to submit an original piece of work to Zurich University. He offered his world-shattering paper on relativity, but it was rejected because it was (as Albert said) 'a little uncanny' (i.e. a bit weird). Luckily, an unweird (but brilliant) paper about atoms did the trick, and he became a Doctor. Albert also decided he wanted a job as a university lecturer. To be on the safe side, Albert submitted ALL his amazing papers with his job application. Together, they covered just about the most important set of scientific advances anyone has ever made. So did he get the job? Well...

The next year, he applied for a job as a maths teacher – and was turned down. Finally, he wrote a special paper on lumpy light for Bern University and he was offered a part-time lecturing job there.

University of Bern

LECTURE ANNOUNCEMENT

SUBJECT: Really tricky physics.

TO BE GIVEN BY: Someone you've never heard of unless you're a top physicist, in which case you know all about really tricky physics already.

START TIME: Saturday, 7a.m. **(THIS IS NOT A MISPRINT)**

Free sleeping bag for first six applicants.

For some inexplicable reason, these lectures weren't all that popular: in fact, the only people who came to them were Albert's sister Maja and three of his friends: two from the Patent Office, and one from the post office. Eventually, Albert did get one real student, but soon after that the others stopped turning up. Imagine being in a class where you're the only student and Albert Einstein is your teacher! What would happen?

Well, what happened in this case was that Albert cancelled the class.

Meanwhile, several people were getting highly excited about relativity theory, and having all sorts of fun with it, applying it to things, checking it, adding twiddly bits to it. In fact, Albert once said...

...since the mathematicians pounced on the relativity theory I no longer understand it.

One of these people was Hermann Minkowski. Hermann was one of Albert's ex-teachers, and he didn't think much of him. (When he heard that it was Albert who'd invented the theory of relativity, he couldn't believe it, and called Albert 'a lazy dog who never bothered about mathematics at all'.) Albert didn't think much of what Hermann did with relativity either, to begin with.

Hermann gave a lecture on relativity and talked about world lines, the postulate of the absolute world and the fourth dimension. Albert wasn't keen on that sort of talk, and said 'the fourth dimension' made him feel especially spooky. After a while, though, Albert got to be quite keen on this strange extra dimension, which we'll explore in the next chapter...

THE FOURTH DIMENSION

What Hermann Minkowski said in his lecture was that really space and time are part of the same thing – a thing that's now called space-time.

Brain Box

Seeing other dimensions

Albert and Hermann are about to explore the fourth dimension, but before they do, it's worth finding out about the other three. They are:

1. Up and down.
2. Left and right.
3. Backwards and forwards (or near and far, or in and out).

Together, these three dimensions make up space. Before we see what it means to live in four dimensions, let's see what life might be like in fewer dimensions...

What would a world be like without the near/far dimension? You're looking at a world like this now – the surface of this page. It's got lines that go up/down:

|

and left/right:

—

and both at once:

/

But no lines go into or out of the paper.

Imagine a Flat Albert living in a two-dimensional world, like a piece of paper.[1]

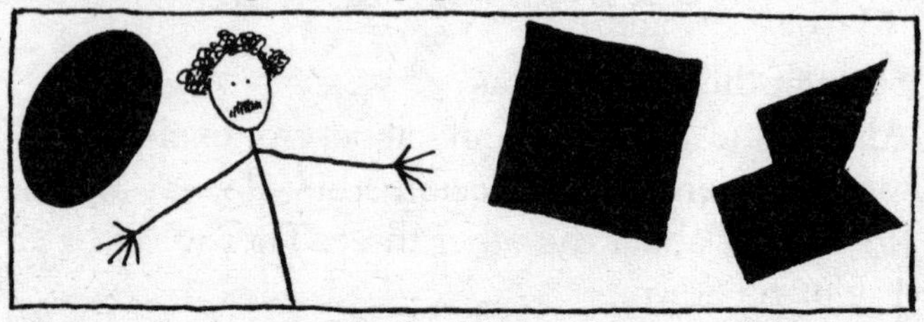

He can look towards the bottom or top of the page or to left or right, but he can't look up out of the flat world (so he can't see you looking down at him). You can see the objects around him as ovals, squares and pointy shapes, but he can't see that: he

1 For more about what life would be like in a 2-dimensional world, read E A Abbot's *Flatland*.

sees them all from the side, so they all just look like lines to him. To see our world a bit like Flat Albert sees his, you could make a narrow horizontal slit in a big piece of cardboard and hold it a few centimetres in front of you. Though the slit, you can see left and right and near and far, but not up and down anymore. Don't fall over that chair...

Although Flat Albert can't see the objects around him like you can, he can look at them from different angles and touch them until he has a good idea of their different shapes. This is what happens in our ordinary space too. If you look at a pedal bin from different angles you can see it as an oblong with flat ends, a shape with two straight sides and two curved ends, or a circle – but you know it's really a cylinder all the time, seen from different angles.

Would Flat Albert ever guess there was a third dimension, even though he could never see it? Maybe he would:

Imagine taking a square tile and pressing one corner through the two-dimensional world.

Flat Albert would see this:

–

If you gradually pressed the tile through Flat Albert's world, he'd see the line get longer and then shorter again like this:

Most flat people would just see a line that mysteriously appeared, lengthened, shortened, and vanished, but, by the way the line changed shape, Flat Albert would cleverly understand that it could be explained by an object from the spooky third dimension passing through his flat world. (If you look through your piece-of-cardboard-with-a-slit-in-it and get someone to move a square shape past it, corner first, you'll see just what Flat Albert would.)

Now, imagine there's a fourth dimension. You can't see it, any more than Flat Albert could see the third one, but if a four-dimensional creature pushed something through our dimension, what would you see? You'd see a solid object that seemed to appear, grow, shrink and vanish again.

This all sounds very mysterious, but if we saw bits of four-dimensional objects every day, we'd get used to them and understand how they work, even though we could never see the whole things. Actually, this is the sort of thing we do anyway. All we ever see of our own world are two-dimensional pictures on the backs of our eyes. We just get used to working out three-dimensional shapes from these two-dimensional pictures (and by feeling the shapes of the objects). And, if you see a picture on TV of an object hurtling 'towards' you, all that's really happening is that its image is growing on the two-dimensional TV screen. We get so used to working out, from two-dimensional views, what three-dimensional objects look like that it's hard not to do it. Look at this:

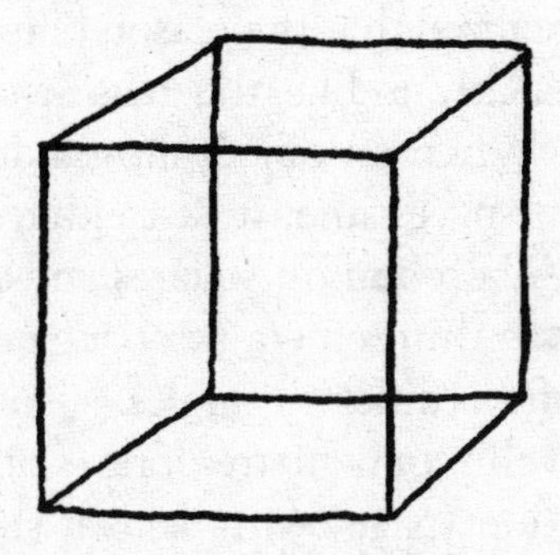

You can choose to see it as a cube seen from above, or a cube seen from below – but it's actually quite tricky to make yourself see it for what it really is – a flat, two-dimensional shape. It just goes to show how easy it is to work out what things are like in a higher dimension!

Hermann suggested that there really was a fourth dimension, but that it was nothing weird or mysterious – it was just time. Together, the three space dimensions and time make up space-time. This idea is a big help in explaining what happens to fast-moving objects.

Imagine holding a javelin in a field on a sunny day. It casts a shadow on the ground – a two-dimensional shadow. How can you change the length of the shadow? Just by holding the javelin at a different angle, you can do it easily. But the javelin's real length doesn't change.

Hermann realized that the reason objects shrink when they move quickly is like the reason shadows change their lengths. When an object moves, it gets shorter in space – but in space-time, it just changes its angle. It's just like Flat Albert and his squares and ovals, or us with our pedal bins – things seem to change shape when you look at them from different angles.

So if a javelin one metre long is thrown at 0.9c, Albert's equation (page 66) tells us it shrinks to 44 cm. At 0.99c, Albert's equation gives the length as 14 cm. The faster the javelin goes, the shorter it becomes – according to us. But if you were a super-fast alien called Flobbo D Lob with hundreds of legs and eyes on stalks who could see things in four-dimensional space-time in the same way we see things in our three-dimensional space, what you'd see wouldn't be a javelin getting shorter as it got faster – you'd just realize that you were seeing the javelin from a different angle. You'd probably feel quite smug about it, and superior to those daft humans with their ridiculously small number of legs and silly ideas.

If we were used to travelling at stunningly high speeds (or, as Flobbo would say, 'just ambling along'), we'd probably get used to this way of looking at things, and it would be just as obvious why a javelin can look 10 cm long as why a pedal bin can look like a circle.

Brain Box

The time dimension

If the idea of time being a dimension seems strange, look back at the picture on page 80, showing the way a square tile looks to Flat Albert as it passes through his two-dimensional world. As you look down the page, you're seeing the tile as it looks to Albert as time passes. You're tracking the tile through the time dimension, which is laid out vertically on the page. Wall-planners and graphs of company profits also show time as a dimension, though they usually lay it out horizontally.

Hermann found that the changes that happen to time can also be explained as shifts in space-time. What Flobbo can see, even with three eyes shut, but which Albert and Hermann had to work out for us humans, is:

SECRETS OF SPACE AND TIME
Number Four: Space and time are linked.

By the way, remember that all this stuff about shrinking depends on the observer – if you were moving with the javelin it wouldn't shrink. This is why it's called relativity – the lengths of objects depend on their speed relative to the observer.

In 1909, Albert was still working in the Patent Office. Though it was fun in a way, he would really much rather have had a proper full-time university job where he could teach advanced students and have plenty of time free for the Universe. So when he heard there was an associate professor's job going at Zurich University in Switzerland, he applied for it. Unfortunately, he wasn't a great teacher – in fact, when the person who had to decide whether to recommend Albert for the job came to see him teach, they had a bit of a shouting match. Luckily the next time they got on much better and finally he did get the job.

(The University wanted to give the job to Albert's friend Friedrich Adler, but he said, 'If it is possible to obtain a man like Einstein for the University, it is absurd to appoint me.' Later on, Albert would return the favour – by saving Friedrich's life.)

When Albert started teaching at Zurich, he wasn't quite what people had expected. He gave his lectures from scribbly notes on a little piece of cardboard, and encouraged the students to ask questions, no matter how silly they were. This was *not* what classes in those days were normally like – the students probably expected to have to sit quietly while lecturers read out from a manuscript. But they soon got used to Albert's technique. Things got even more relaxed when Albert took them all to a local café to continue their lesson there.

Albert enjoyed these lessons, but he wasn't keen on the practical ones – he said, 'I scarcely dare to pick up a piece of apparatus for fear it might blow up.'

He didn't teach relativity, but he did give a talk about it to a scientific society. After a long discussion about time, he discovered he hadn't brought his watch with him and, having just told his audience what time was, he had to ask them what time it was.

Soon after this, Albert explained why the sky is blue! (Sadly, the publisher says this book's quite long enough already, without taking extra pages to explain how he did it. It was jolly clever though.)

For most scientists, this would have been enough to retire on, but for Albert it was only part of a project of his which he'd started in 1905 – he wanted to prove that atoms exist. To us, living in the twenty-first century, this doesn't seem to need proving any more than the Earth being round does. But lots of scientists in Albert's day didn't believe in them. Some thought atoms were just some sort of unit, like hours or metres – a useful idea, but not a real physical thing. So how did Albert prove they were real? As only a genius could: he gave no fewer than seven ways of working out how big atoms must be, based on things like the thickness of syrup, the behaviour of light – and the blueness of the sky.

Since all the ways gave the same answer for the size of an atom, people just had to believe there were such things. The only disappointing thing is the titles of the papers. Instead of…

SECRETS OF THE ATOM REVEALED!!!

Or even…

ATOMS: YES OR NO?

They were called things like:

On the Motion of Small Particles Suspended in a Stationary Liquid, according to the Molecular Kinetic Theory of Heat

But everyone loved them just the same.

Albert's European tour

After a couple of years, Albert moved up from being an Associate Professor, and became a full one. Not only that, he got a lot richer too. This was partly because an unknown admirer gave him a big pile of cash, just for being such a great scientist (not the sort of thing that happens too often, but perhaps it helped that Albert was such a nice bloke as well, unlike certain other geniuses we could mention).

The only thing was, the Professorship was in Prague. Albert's arrival wasn't brilliant – he was so scruffy that the University porter thought he'd come to fix the lights. And things went downhill from there...

ALBERT'S LOST NOTEBOOK

Four things I hate about Prague:

1. You can't drink the water.
2. The bedbugs are enormous.
3. I can't speak Czech.
4. The Czechs don't like Germans. (I keep trying to tell them I'm not German, but see 3.)

Albert had to attend massive meetings with the other professors, which were full of internal politics and back-stabbing. This got on his nerves, though he did once say...

But two nice things happened to Albert in Prague. He and Mileva had a son called Eduard and, in 1911, he was invited to the first Solvay conference. Solvay was a really rich bloke with his own theories about gravity – which were a little bit on the odd side. The other scientists were much happier talking to each other about *their* theories than listening to Solvay's, but he can't have minded too much, because he kept his conferences going for years.

The conference was stuffed full of brain-power. In fact just about everyone who was anyone in science was there, including Max Planck and the dead famous Marie Curie. They were all a bit edgy just then because of what was happening to a new area of science which was later called quantum theory, which we'll get round to on page 150. Albert had helped invent it a few years earlier, and it hadn't been too popular then on account of its mind-scrambling weirdness, but that was nothing to how strange it had become by 1911, by which point even Albert wasn't happy with it. (You can't wait to reach page 150, can you?) Anyway, it was great fun for Albert to meet so many scientists, and everyone liked him.

The next year, Albert met up with his cousin Elsa. They hadn't seen each other since they were children together in Munich, but they got on very well indeed. In fact Elsa wrote him love letters, sending them secretly to the University, and making sure Albert burnt them. After all, Albert was still married to Mileva, even though neither of them was very happy about it.

Albert never did get to like Prague, and when he got the chance of another professorship, back at the Poly, he jumped at it.

Albert didn't drink alcohol because it interfered with solving the mysteries of the Universe, but he did smoke a pipe. Unfortunately the Poly's attitude on smoking was tough. Well, tough-*ish*.

This made Albert extra popular, if unhealthy.

One of Albert's visitors at Zurich was Marie Curie, who brought her daughter Eve with her. They went for hikes in the mountains, taking Albert's sons Hans and Eduard with them, and talked non-stop about science – at one point Albert grabbed Marie excitedly and shouted: 'I need to know exactly what happens in a lift when it falls into space.'

You'll have noticed that Mileva wasn't up the mountain chatting about lifts as well. It was about then that Albert realized that things were going badly wrong with their marriage. They no longer talked about science as they used to, and Mileva's unpopularity with Albert's family didn't help.

You'd think Albert would be nicely settled in Zurich – plenty of money, pretty countryside, lots of science, nice smoky office. But, now he was famous, everyone was keen to have him at their university so they could show him off. The Prussian Academy in Berlin made Albert a very attractive offer – loads of money, the directorship of an Institute of Theoretical Physics, and a Professorship at the Friderich-Wilhelm University. In exchange, all Albert had to do was live in Berlin and turn up at meetings from time to time. Albert didn't really want to go back to Germany, but two of his friends, Max Planck and Walther Nernst, managed to persuade him. So in 1913 Albert moved yet *again*, this time to Berlin. He'd only been in Zurich two years.

Albert was happy in Berlin, despite being back in Germany, having to dress smartly, and going to meetings where everyone lectured on their own subject while everyone else fell asleep. But Mileva hated it, and before long she went back to Zurich and took Hans and Eduard with her. Five years later, in 1919, she and Albert were divorced, and not long after, Albert married

Elsa. It took a long time for Mileva to get over the break-up, but they did eventually become reasonably friendly again.

It was 1913 when Albert arrived in Berlin. The next year:

NEWS OF THE UNIVERSE

6 November 1914

WAR!

The bad news

For the last few years, many countries have been building up their military forces and trying to extend their empires. Following the murder of the Austrian Arch-duke Ferdinand and his wife on 28 June this year by a Serbian assassin in Sarajevo, Austria-Hungary declared war on Serbia. A series of declarations of war followed, with Germany, Austria-Hungary and Turkey on one side and Britain, France, Serbia, North Africa and Russia on the other. Other countries are likely to take sides soon, until most of the world is at war.

The good news

It will all be over by Christmas.

But it wasn't. The First World War (then called the Great War) lasted until November 1918, and over nine million people were killed. An especially horrible feature of the war was that machine-guns had been invented by then, but tanks hadn't, at least not to begin with. So thousands of unprotected men would run across the battlefield to attack machine-gun emplacements. Almost all of them would be slaughtered, until a few got through to kill the machine-gunners. But then there would be other lines of machine-guns to deal with, at the cost of even more lives. It's not surprising that Albert was disgusted by it. He'd always hated conflict of any sort – even in sports – so he was completely opposed to the war.

However, lots of Albert's friends thought the war was a great idea. Soon after Germany invaded Belgium, some of them even signed a statement that appeared in newspapers all over the world called an 'Appeal to the Cultured World'. It said – which certainly wasn't true – that German soldiers hadn't killed a single Belgian during their invasion. It had 93 signatures from leading Germans, including Albert's friends Max and Walther, the ones who'd talked him into returning to Germany.

What could Albert do? For the first time in his life he did something political: he collaborated on a reply to the 'Appeal to the Cultured World'...

APPEAL TO EUROPEANS

In reply to the recent *Appeal to the Cultured World*, the undersigned wish to point out that:

a) no one ever really wins in war
b) Europe should be more united, not less.

But only four people signed it.

Albert did lots more things to try to stop the war, including smuggling anti-war papers, trying to organize an anti-war book with articles from scientists on both sides, and helping people who were in trouble for objecting to the war. He argued for peace over and over again. But no one listened to him.

It might seem strange, but Albert didn't fall out with even the most war-loving scientists. But then Albert's relationships with people were often a bit distant – he cared less about individuals than about humanity as a whole. Also, he always tried to take an objective, long-term view of things. He realized that the war wouldn't last forever, and wanted science to be as unaffected by it as possible. For that to happen, scientists would have to keep talking to each other, no matter what side they were on.

Even so, it's still hard to understand how he managed. For instance, one of his friends, Fritz Haber, invented all sorts of deadly gases, and supervised the production of chlorine, which killed or wounded 15,000 soldiers in a single attack. But Albert still stayed matey with him. Another thing that's a bit odd is that Albert himself helped the war effort. He didn't do anything too terrible – just helping to develop a special type of compass for use in submarines, and trying to design better aircraft wings. Of course, planes and submarines aren't only used in war, but Albert must have realized that his work – if it was any good – would help to make the German air force and navy stronger, which he was definitely opposed to.

In 1916 an old friend of Albert's, Friedrich Adler, turned up again. Remember him? He was the left-wing student at the Poly, who turned down the professorship at Prague so that Albert would get it. Although Albert knew that his friend had always been a little bit fanatical about politics, even he must have been surprised when he heard that Friedrich had assassinated the Austrian leader, Count Karl Stürgkh, because he'd got rid of the parliament and taken personal control of the country. Friedrich was facing execution but Albert and others convinced the court that he was really a good bloke on the whole, who should be sent to prison instead.

But it wasn't all science and politics for Albert – he joined a Literary Society of writers for tea and cigars each week. He got a bit tired of being asked to explain his theories though...

Peace?

Albert spent a lot of time and energy working and fighting for peace, but almost none looking after himself. By the beginning of 1917, he was ill with stomach and liver problems and an ulcer.

He was never very convinced by medical science – he said the only way to tell what was wrong with someone was to wait until they were dead and them cut then up to see what the problem had been. Luckily for the world, not to mention Albert, that wasn't necessary – instead he was sent on holiday to the Baltic coast for eight weeks. He spent his time lying on the beach ('like a crocodile' he said, but he didn't actually bite anyone's leg off as far as anyone knows).

He also discovered how much he enjoyed not wearing shoes and socks. From then on he avoided them –

especially socks – whenever possible, even when he was dead famous and went to posh dinners.

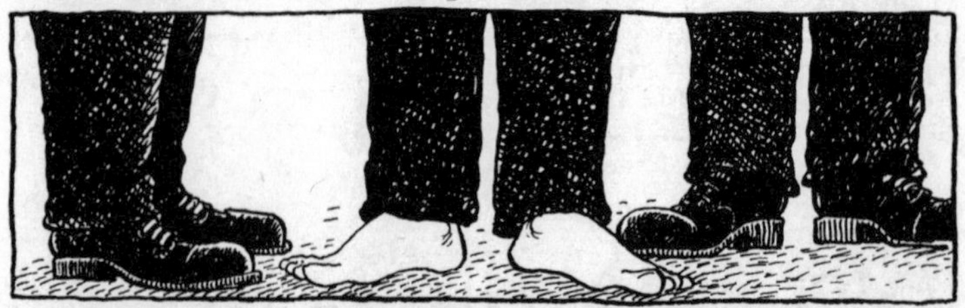

Albert wasn't the only one who was ill just then; Mileva and Eduard were too. And they needed money. So he gave them some, and promised them all the dosh that went with his Nobel Prize too.

Sure enough, four years later Albert got the prize and gave Mileva the money.

During the autumn of 1918 Albert gave regular lectures on relativity, until, on 4 November, he wrote in his lecture notebook

Class cancelled due to revolution.

And it was. Not like the French one when everyone got their head cut off, but a revolution all the same. Everyone was sick of the war, and when they realized they were going to lose even though all their leaders had been saying they were on the verge of winning, lots of people joined together and organized a huge strike and mass demonstrations demanding peace. Albert loved it – and people loved him too, now that they'd done what he'd been telling them to do for the last four years. He was so popular that he even managed to persuade some revolting students to release some professors they'd locked up.

Finally...

NEWS OF THE UNIVERSE

11 November 1918

WAR IS OVER!

At 5 a.m. today Germany at last surrendered to Allied Forces.

NEWS OF THE UNIVERSE

28 June 1919

TREATY SIGNED

In an historic meeting today, in the presence of thirty nations, a treaty was signed in Versailles, France. The treaty states that:

- The war was all Germany's fault and no one else had anything to do with it.
- All Germany's colonies, and some of its European territory, is now the property of the victors (which isn't stealing, honest).
- Germany has to pay compensation to absolutely everyone.

With everything sorted out so reasonably, there should never be another world war.

So, after four terrible years, the war was finally over. Though Albert, like everyone else, had found it extremely depressing, it hadn't stopped him working: he found it quite easy to switch off from what was going on around him, and think about science instead. He loved retreating to the attic for a nice bit of thinking, where he worried about being neat and tidy even less than usual (which was quite an achievement). According to one of his visitors, he looked like...

When he didn't have any particular mystery of the Universe to solve, Albert was quite happy to think through tricky mathematical proofs, just for fun. But in fact he *did* have a proper bit of science to work on just then. It was the most amazing bit of science anyone has ever done.

You may be wondering why Albert's theory is called SPECIAL relativity. It's not because it's wonderful (even though it is), but because it only works in the special situation where you're moving smoothly in a straight line, which is where the Principle of Relativity applies. What Albert wanted next was something that would work with any sort of movement – wobbling, speeding up, slowing down, spinning in circles until you're sick – a GENERAL theory of relativity.

In Special Relativity, Albert had shown that there is no way to tell whether you're moving smoothly or not, and this had led him to amazing discoveries about light, time and space. Now he wanted to extend the theory so that it could cope with *all* motion, not just the smooth sort. This would mean that whenever anyone said…

… an irritating scientist could always pop up and say …

This is a weird idea. In fact, it sounds impossible. Surely you can say for sure if your train has jerked to a halt or your bike has just gone from 0 to 60 in five seconds? Yet for Albert to show that all motion is relative, he'd have to be able to show that you might be wrong about such things. He'd have to be stupendously brainy to do that!

Fortunately, he was.

He was sitting in his office one day when the answer came to him – he called it his happiest thought. The thought was:

In other words, if you're falling, you can't feel the pull of gravity. In fact, to simulate the weightless conditions encountered in space travel, NASA uses special planes to train its astronauts. The planes fly very high and then drop down towards the Earth. So long as the planes fall, the astronauts feel no gravity. Now this is really very odd. If something pulls you, you can usually feel it, because your body has a natural resistance (called its inertia) to being pulled around. If you can't feel the pull of gravity when you're falling, it can only mean that the pull is exactly right to cancel your inertia. Experiments had shown that this was really true – the two forces were of *exactly* the same strength. Yet, until Albert, no one knew why this should be.

So Albert decided to assume that whatever gravity could do, acceleration could do too – and vice versa. This is another one of those ideas like 'The laws of physics are the same whether you're moving or not' that seem so obvious you don't know quite what to do with them. But Albert knew.

SCARY SCIENCE WARNING

There is a certain amount of simple maths involved in General Relativity. Relatively simple. Well, actually, quite a lot of quite complicated maths. Oh all right, an enormous amount of mind-chillingly, nightmarishly, terrifyingly difficult maths. BUT the good news is, a lot of General Relativity can be understood with no maths at all, so there's none in this section. Not so much as a single $(x–y)^5$. And, though some of the ideas themselves are a bit tricky, there's a summary on page 117.

Let's think about a train and the Principle of Relativity again. What Albert had to do was to show that the Principle works whatever the train does. In other words, he had to show that there's no way a passenger on the train can tell it's really moving – even if it's jerking or turning or speeding up or slowing down or wobbling or crashing.

Now, the thing about all these types of motion is that you can *feel* them happening. Those sensations of speeding up or slowing down or wishing you hadn't eaten all those burgers tell you what's going on. (From now on, we'll lump all these types of motion together under the heading of 'acceleration'.) If the Principle of Relativity was going to work for acceleration, Albert needed to show that something else could cause those sensations. And now he knew what that was, thanks to his happiest thought. The something else was gravity.

How could Albert get to grips with gravity and acceleration? If gravity could do whatever acceleration could, then a light ray must behave in just the same way in a room that stands on the surface of the Earth as in one that accelerates dramatically upwards. And what does light do in an accelerating room? It curves, as another thought-experiment shows:

Let's imagine Terry and Val are two super-athletic people who are used to running about at nearly the speed of light. Val has a powerful laser, mounted on a tripod because it's heavy. Terry has three economy-size jellies on plates.

To begin with, Val fires the laser at the first jelly, which Terry holds still. The laser beam, which seems to move quite slowly to such speedy people, makes its way to the jelly, and drills a hole right through it. The hole looks like this:

Now, Terry takes the second jelly (it's a lime one this time), and holds it up while Val fires the laser again. As the beam melts its way through the jelly, Terry raises it, so the edge of the melted area is a sloping line:

This line is a handy record of the progress of the laser-beam through the lime jelly.

Next they try something more complicated. As Val fires the laser a third time, Terry raises the final jelly, a lemon one with a hint of blackcurrant, but this time, he starts off moving it slowly and gradually speeds up – that is, he *accelerates* it. And now the edge of the melted bit is a curve:

That all boils down to two things:

- the path of a laser-beam (or any other light-ray) in an accelerating jelly (or room) is curved;
- a nice fruity smell.

So Albert realised that acceleration makes light curve. But if acceleration and gravity have the same effects, *gravity* must make light curve too, just as it curves water jets:

Recently the Hubble Space Telescope has found all sorts of weird light patterns caused by light curving near heavy objects. There are even some called Einstein Crosses. The first one to be found looks like five stars in a cross shape, but is actually just ONE star, with its light curved all over the place by a galaxy.

The idea that light can curve doesn't sound too amazing to begin with. But, just as with Special Relativity, an apparently simple idea was to lead to incredible things when Albert followed the logic through.

Holding back time

Imagine there's a huge furry ball rolling past you really quickly in a straight line and you grab at it. You just catch hold of some of its fur, but you're not strong enough to stop it, and it pulls itself away and keeps going. What happens to its direction? It will divert slightly – just like light does when it passes the sun.

But that's not all – you'll also slow the ball down. And that's just what gravity does to light: it makes it curve *and* slows it down. But if light slows down, so do light-clocks, and Albert already knew (from Special Relativity) what that meant:

SECRETS OF SPACE AND TIME
Number Five:
GRAVITY SLOWS TIME DOWN.

Like all relativity effects, this one is very small for most of us. The gravity on the Earth's surface only slows down clocks by about a second a century, but this tiny effect has been measured – clocks sent round the Earth on jet planes have been found to speed up a teeny bit of a tick, because the planes fly far above the Earth, where the pull of gravity is weaker.

The Sun's gravity is much greater than Earth's, but it's still a bit wimpish. OK, it's true that you'd weigh a tonne and a half if you stood on the Sun's surface. (Except you can't because **a**) it's 5,500°C and **b**) it hasn't got one[1]).

But that's nothing to show off about as far as gravity goes. The Sun just slightly disturbs the paths of light rays that pass it, and just slightly slows down time – by about a minute a year.

But there are less wimpy things in space, things that Albert had never heard of, called black holes. In fact they're quite scary. They don't just bend light, they pull it in completely so it can never escape. And they don't

1 Because it's made of gas.

just slow time down – they stop it. It's just as if you were strong enough to hold on to that furry ball that was rolling past.

If you watched someone approach a black hole in a spaceship, you'd see the ship get slower and slower. If you had a good enough telescope, you'd see the person inside slow down too, and their clocks tick more slowly. If the person hung around the black hole for a while and then returned to you, you'd find less time had passed for them than for you.

This could be very weird. If your parents went to a black hole for their 2010 summer holidays, they'd age more slowly than you, so that when they came home, they could be younger than you! According to you their holiday might have lasted for twenty years, while according to them it might have lasted only a week – but when they returned home they'd find it was 2030.

So Albert had discovered a way to travel in time – all you need is *lots* of stuff (anything will do) to squash together to make a nice strong gravity-field with, and a vehicle that can take you in and out of the gravity-field. But there's just one problem with using this as a time-machine – although you can travel into the future, you can't get back to your own time again, because you can't travel into the past. (There might just be a way to do that though, as we'll see later on).

But this was only one of Albert's amazing discoveries:

The Secret of Spinning

Imagine a bicycle wheel spinning round and round in space at half the speed of light. Because the tyre is moving so fast it must get shorter (Secret Three: Moving Things Shrink). And a shorter tyre means a smaller wheel. But what about the spokes? They're moving too, but only sideways, so they don't get shorter, just thinner. But if they stay the same length, the wheel must stay the same size. How can the wheel get smaller and yet stay the same size? Does this mean there's something wrong with Special Relativity?

OK, so it's not Special Relativity's job to explain this. But General Relativity *is* supposed to deal with non-smooth motion – so can *it* explain it?

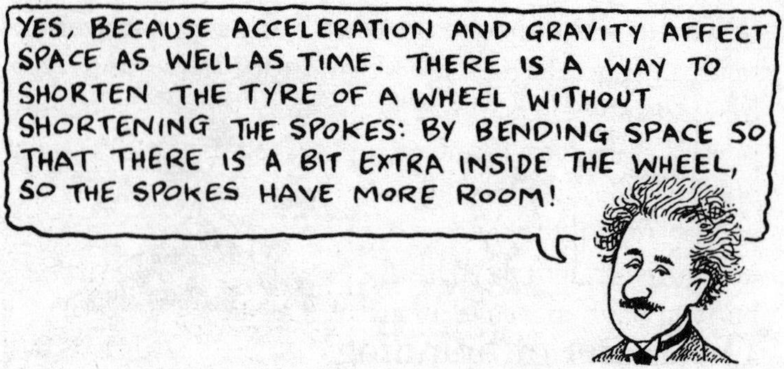

YES, BECAUSE ACCELERATION AND GRAVITY AFFECT SPACE AS WELL AS TIME. THERE IS A WAY TO SHORTEN THE TYRE OF A WHEEL WITHOUT SHORTENING THE SPOKES: BY BENDING SPACE SO THAT THERE IS A BIT EXTRA INSIDE THE WHEEL, SO THE SPOKES HAVE MORE ROOM!

Albert was sure that all the effects of gravity could be explained by bent, curved, twisted or otherwise mangled space. In fact, he soon realised that there was no need to talk about matter causing gravity and gravity curving space. Instead, he could simply say:

SECRETS OF SPACE AND TIME
Number Six:
MATTER BENDS SPACE.

So Albert had found that matter slows time and bends space: in other words, it curves (or distorts or bends or warps) space-time.

The idea of curved space-time came in very handy! Left to themselves, light-rays or moving objects travel in straight lines. But when there are things like planets and stars about, their masses bend space-time. So things just *can't* go straight anymore – they have to follow the curves of space-time, just like a train has to follow the curves of its rails.

It's as if you dug rings around you in the sand on the beach, so any beach balls going by would tend to curve round you: not because you grabbed them, but because of what you'd done to the sand. Or imagine one day a really untidy relative called Ermintrude moves into your house, and covers the living-room floor in suitcases, piles of clothes and stuffed leopards, before falling asleep on the sofa. All this stuff means you can't walk straight across the floor anymore. You go as straight as you can, but you have to weave about a bit (muttering to yourself a lot) to stick to the clear areas. But Ermintrude isn't pulling you off course herself – it's what she's done to the room that affects you.

So Albert had discovered another secret of the Universe:

SECRETS OF SPACE AND TIME
Number Seven:
LIGHT AND MATTER FOLLOW THE SHAPE OF SPACE-TIME.

Trouble with maths

Albert was only halfway to a proper theory. He understood that matter must change time and space, so now he just had to find out how to do the sums that would tell him how much. But he couldn't.

The problem is that if matter curves space, it will also curve any instrument you put into the space to measure how curvy it is: diagrams like the one on page 59 are fine for working out what happens to things in Special Relativity, but General Relativity is like tearing out that page and screwing it up and saying 'OK, now use the diagram to work out the crumpliness of the paper.' But of course you can't because the diagram is just part of the crumple... It's all very tricky. Describing physical laws without geometry is, as Albert said, 'similar to describing our thoughts without words'.

So Albert asked his friends to help. He once burst into his friend Marcel Grossman's house saying, 'You've got to help me, or I'll go mad!' Since Albert was finding it impossible to get anywhere using ordinary geometry, Marcel suggested he used something else: Bernhard Riemann had worked out a fiendishly tricky geometry years before, when he was doing some fascinating work on how metal plates go all bendy when you heat them up, and Marcel thought Albert might find it handy for his fiendishly tricky sums. And so it was.

SCARY SCIENCE WARNING

I lied on page 104. There are two equations coming up, but only to look at.

It took Albert several years and plenty of help from Marcel before he nailed down the maths he wanted. It turned out to be very complicated maths indeed. For instance, according to Isaac Newton a really really simple object like a tiny spherical mass has a gravity pull like this:

But according to Albert, you have to talk about curved space-time instead of gravity-pull, so you end up with equations like this:

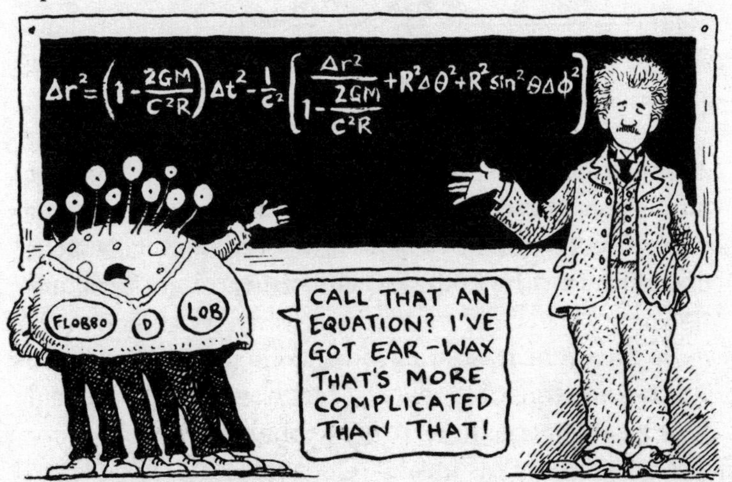

But now Albert had another problem: once you give up on normal geometry, there are lots of different answers to a question. For instance, the area of a circle is normally just given by πr^2. So a bicycle wheel with spokes 50cm long has an area of about $3.1416 \times 50 \times 50$, which is about 8,000 cm^2. But in the geometry Albert had to use, the area could have all sorts of values: there are all sorts of ways to curve and stretch space to fit the non-shortened spokes inside a shortened tyre, just like there are lots of ways to squash a plasticene star into a matchbox.

So, how could Albert choose the right way to describe the way space-time actually curved?

Well, for a start, Isaac Newton was a big help. His laws worked brilliantly in almost every situation. So Albert's equations had to give more or less the same answers as

Isaac's, because, for the world we're used to Isaac was very very nearly right!

Actually Isaac's equations had only been known to fail with the motion of the planet Mercury. So Albert had to explain everything just as well as Isaac, and it would be ever so nice if he could explain the motion of Mercury too.

So Albert at least knew how to check the answers his space-time equations gave – but how could he decide which sort of equations to try in the first place?

This is where his idea of 'God' came in. He reckoned 'God' would choose the simplest equations – so Albert tried them and they worked! The answers he got fitted with Isaac's predictions, AND explained the motion of Mercury too. Mind you, the equations Albert had to choose from were all a bit on the nightmarishly complicated side, so even the simplest ones would make most people a bit edgy. But never mind. Albert was incredibly happy for days. It was his greatest triumph, probably THE greatest triumph of any scientist ever. He had formulated the equations that describe motion, gravity, time, space and energy in terms of curved space-time. He was soon to discover that they could even explain the Universe itself.

Using General Relativity, Albert was also able to explain the odd fact that, according to Isaac's law, gravity takes no time to travel – which is the same thing as saying it travels infinitely fast. But Albert had always said nothing could go faster than light! What General Relativity showed him was that gravity travels at the speed of light – in waves.

Although almost all scientists believe in gravity waves these days, and have built huge detectors to measure them, so far no one's found any. In 1987 a massive star in the next-door galaxy went BOOMMMMMMM!!!!!!

It would have been a lovely thing for the gravity-wave detectors to measure, but sadly all three happened to be switched off at the time.

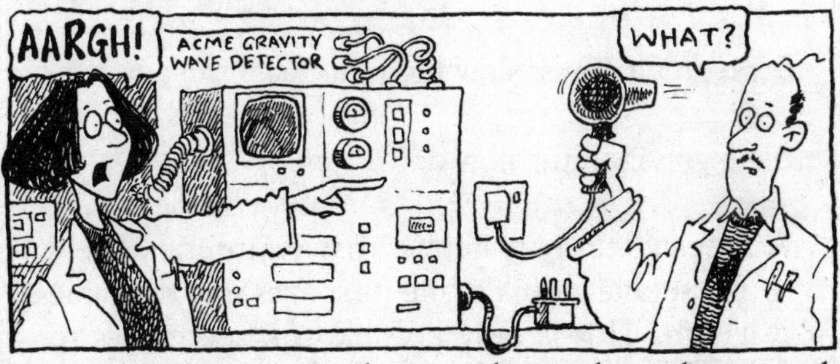

General Relativity is a huge and complex subject, and people are still working on it. But it's all based on the rules Albert worked out.

NEW! FUN-SIZE!

EINSTEIN'S EINCREDIBLE THEORIES
GENERAL RELATIVITY

1 Special Relativity could only show that it isn't possible to know you're moving smoothly. Albert wanted to show you couldn't even know for sure that you're accelerating. Also, the law of gravity didn't really fit with Special Relativity.

2. Albert solved both these problems when he realized that the pull of gravity feels just like an acceleration. So he decided whatever gravity could do, acceleration could do too (and vice versa).

3. Acceleration makes light curve. So gravity must make it curve too.

4. If gravity makes light curve, it must also slow it down.

5. So gravity must slow light-clocks.

6. So gravity must slow down time.

7. Special Relativity implies that a spinning wheel's tyre should shrink while its spokes stay the same length. This is only possible if space curves to accommodate the spokes. So spinning (which is a type of acceleration as far as relativity is concerned) curves space.

8. Whatever acceleration does, gravity does too. Therefore, gravity must also curve space.

9. In fact, gravity *is* just the distortion (or curve or warp or bend) that matter makes in space and time.

Albert was very happy with General Relativity and was quite certain it was right, but it's always nice to have these things proved, if only so you can say...

Albert had shown that when light passes near the Sun it must curve. This means that as the Sun moves across the sky it bends the light from the stars it seems to pass close to (it doesn't really get anywhere near them of course – it's just that their light comes close to the Sun on its way to our eyes). So all you have to do is look at the stars that are really close to the Sun and see if they seem to be in slightly different places to where they are when the Sun's not there. Easy, isn't it? Except of course there aren't too many stars around in the daytime.

So why not look at the stars near the Sun during an eclipse?

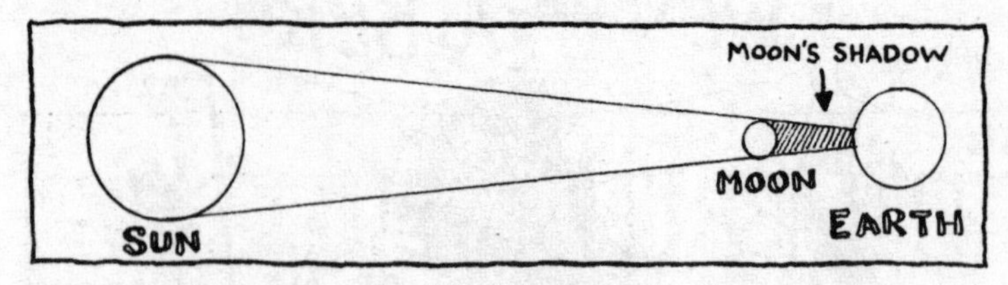

Albert wanted to try this during the 1914 eclipse, but the First World War got in the way. Happily there was another one coming up soon – in 1919 in fact – and what was extra handy was that this particular eclipse would take place in front of a whole mass of little stars called the Hyades. How exciting! In 1917, Albert's fellow scientists decided to take the opportunity to find out what stars near the Sun get up to when we we're not looking, even though a) the eclipse would only be visible from tropical parts of the world and b) the First World War hadn't finished yet.

Two expeditions were planned. One of them was led by Arthur Eddington. Arthur was a top British scientist, who was so startlingly clever he understood relativity theory inside out and upside down. Albert liked Arthur, both because he was exceptionally clever and because he was a pacifist. Arthur refused to fight in the war and was allowed not to by the government, what with him being a top genius and everything, so he'd be around to lead the exciting eclipse expedition (to a little island called Principe off the coast of West Africa) whether the war was finished or not. Meanwhile, other scientists planned to go to Sobral in Brazil, in case Africa was cloudy that day.

Scientists hoped that the 1919 eclipse would prove that Albert was right (or wrong). Albert didn't think of himself as cleverer than Isaac Newton, just that he had a better starting point. But some people saw it a bit differently...

THE BRITISH BULLDOG

5 November 1919

SCIENCE PUNCH-UP

The gloves are off in the big fight between scrambled egg-head Albert Einstein and all-round wonderful bloke Isaac Newton. Following two daring expeditions by British scientists to remote, not to say foreign, corners of the world, photographs have been taken which show the positions of the stars during an eclipse of the Sun.

The photographs are now being analysed. Einstein thinks the Sun's gravity warps space and time, which changes the direction of starlight passing near the Sun. This would mean the photos will show the stars in different positions from usual. Isaac Newton wasn't available for comment, but we know he'd disagree with Einstein's figures. Tomorrow is the big day – at a boffins' conference at the Royal Society in London, the results will be announced and we'll find out who was right. We're backing Isaac.

On page 5: win a cuddly Isaac Newton doll in our 'Back to traditional science' campaign.

On November 6, neither Albert nor Isaac were at the conference. Albert didn't go because he knew he was right, and Isaac didn't go because he'd been dead for three hundred years. As will be no surprise to you, Albert's predictions were confirmed.[1] This wasn't a surprise to a lot of scientists either, since the result had been around for weeks, but the conference was the event at which it was officially accepted by the Royal Society, and it got lots of publicity.

An excited discussion followed the announcement, in which lots of people said they didn't understand relativity. In fact Ludwig Silberstein, who reckoned he understood it but thought it was wrong, said...

(Which was a bit nasty to poor old Silberstein.)

1 Or so it was thought at the time. Actually, the results weren't really accurate enough to be sure.

The next day Albert became … DEAD FAMOUS.

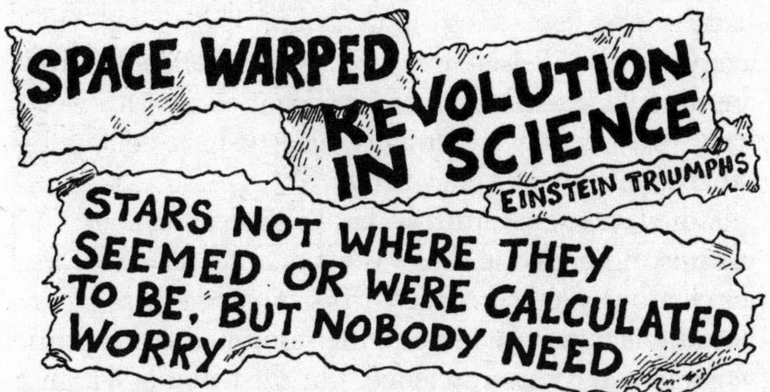

Albert had been famous-ish in Germany for a while, but he was almost unknown anywhere else and now suddenly the papers all over the world were full of him. For a little while Albert didn't know he was a superstar, but he couldn't help noticing something was going on, especially when the *Illustrated Berlin Times* had a huge photo of him on the cover, with the headline: 'A New Giant in World History'.

Albert never really understood what all the fuss was about. Years later, when he met Charlie Chaplin and the crowd was cheering them wildly, Charlie said:

Maybe he was right. Perhaps people liked Albert because he seemed so much more advanced than everyone else – as if they were seeing someone from another planet, full of super-intelligent aliens with weird hair. Anyway, it was certainly nice to have something other than the war to talk about.

Albert soon got quite good at being dead famous, and it came in handy too. He was good at it because he was witty, attractive and modest (sort of), and it was handy because it meant people listened to him – and not just when he talked about science. The First World War had convinced Albert that peace was worth fighting for.

Being famous certainly meant Albert's lectures were popular – there was soon almost no room for students, because all sorts of people would come to watch Albert lecture, chat loudly about how clever he was, pride themselves on not being able to understand relativity and wander off again. In the end, the students complained, and got their lecture fees back.

Fame also meant *lots* of travelling, to lecture about relativity:

During his travels, Albert heard something that would have been a terrible blow to a less confident man:

another scientist called Dayton Miller had apparently discovered that the speed of light varied depending on the motion of the Earth. If the speed of light wasn't constant after all, that meant that the whole of relativity theory was wrong. It was a bit like someone telling Isaac Newton that apples fall upwards, but Albert didn't believe a word of it. Politely, he just said that God was subtle but not malicious – in other words, the Universe wasn't easy to understand, but it *did* make sense whereas Dayton's results didn't! (Dayton was proved wrong later, of course.)

While he was off enjoying himself in Japan, Albert was awarded the Nobel Prize – just as he'd known he would be four years earlier, when he'd promised Mileva the money that went with it. But the Prize wasn't for relativity. It was only awarded at all after a lot of fuss by the officials: they knew Albert was a genius because famous scientists kept writing to tell them so, but the experts they got to check that relativity theory was a major contribution to science weren't too sure, probably because they didn't understand it. Also, the Nobel Prize was supposed to be for practical work. So the committee played it safe and awarded Albert the prize for his work on lumpy light, which deserved it too and which we'll get round to a bit later.

But fame didn't just mean fun and travel for Albert. It meant danger too.

Political Albert

Berlin wasn't a very calm place after the revolution, and in March 1920 there was a counter-revolution when the military tried to re-establish power. The new government had to hide and there was lots of violence. Although this calmed down after a few days, there was still a lot of hatred in Berlin – and some was directed against Albert, as a famous Jew, and someone who had supported the revolution. A group was set up, calling itself The Working Party of German Scientists for the Preservation of a Pure Science, but it should have been called the Anti-Albert Society. Albert himself called it the Anti-Relativity Company Incorporated – when he was being polite. The Society paid people to rubbish relativity theory.

Albert's friends, and lots of other scientists, complained about the Society and said a lot of nice things about Albert, but it didn't do much good. It did even less good when Albert wrote a snappy article replying to the Society in a Berlin newspaper, calling its members bedbugs. Everyone was a bit shocked that Albert hadn't been more laid-back about the whole thing – but then they didn't have to cope with a Society specially invented to be nasty to them.

Why did Albert's Jewishness make some people hate him? It's a sad fact that Jews had been unpopular in many countries for hundreds of years (when Albert was born, they were only allowed to have a very few types of job, which would have kept his ancestors from becoming scientists, however clever they were). They had different customs from other people, and just being different was enough to make some people dislike them. In Germany in the early 1930s these feelings were seized on and stirred up by a political party called the National Socialists – or Nazis. But the fact that Albert was brilliant, popular and Jewish contradicted their propaganda that Jews were terrible. So they just had to discredit him.

It was only about then that being Jewish started to matter to Albert. For him, it had nothing to do with God, but a lot to do with being a member of what he called a tribe. One thing that made Albert care about Jewish problems was that, after the First World War, a large number of Jews settled on the edge of Berlin. They'd escaped from many years of persecution in Russia and Poland and were extremely poor. Some people – including some Jews – wanted to get rid of the new settlers, but Albert wrote an article in a newspaper saying that they should be allowed to stay.

Now that Albert was dead famous he was really useful for Jewish groups, and the World Zionist Organization invited him to go to America to raise funds and publicize the problems of the Jews. Jews hadn't had a country of their own for centuries, and the World Zionist

Organization thought it was about time they did. Albert thought that having different countries was 'the measles of the human race', and that it led to war, so he wasn't all that keen on having yet another one. He didn't like the idea of a being a living poster either, but he accepted the invitation in the hope that it would help the Jews.

Albert even travelled to England and France, though he knew Germans weren't popular there, so soon after the war. But he was such a nice bloke, as well as being the greatest scientist in the world, that he made friends wherever he went. The fact that he had plenty of enemies too didn't worry him, until the German Foreign Minister, Walther Rathenau, was shot.

Walther had been a friend of Albert's, and Albert had even warned him that it would be dangerous to take the Foreign Minister job. Walther had been killed at least partly because he was a famous Jew – might Albert be next? Albert thought so. He cancelled all public appearances and fled from Berlin for a while. Without telling Albert, Elsa secretly organized for the police to protect him, so little groups of secret agents trailed round after him wherever he went (which must have made him a bit edgy if he noticed).

Though Albert soon regained his usual calm and went back to Berlin again, he still avoided meetings, including one in which all sorts of nasty things were said about him, such as that he just used scientific problems to start personal arguments (which was just what the Anti-Relativity Company had been doing to him!). This was the sort of thing Adolf Hitler was saying too: that the Jews were using science for 'a deliberate, systematic poisoning of our nation's soul and thus ... the triggering of the inner collapse of our nation.' (Even Albert couldn't have made sense of that theory).

Just when Albert thought it was safe to go out again, he heard of another death threat and had to hide once more. Not surprisingly, this was *really* starting to get on his nerves, and he was tempted to move to America – but not just for a bit of peace. Exciting research work was being done there, using giant telescopes to investigate the structure of the Universe. Albert had come up with his own theory about this many years before, but as usual it took ages for technology to catch up with him. Let's just nip back to 1917 and see what he discovered.

ALBERT'S INFLATABLE UNIVERSE

Cosmology is the study of the whole Universe (or 'cosmos'). Before Albert came along, it wasn't much of a subject. Philosophers had various ideas about the Universe, but they didn't have any proper theories that could be tested and used to make predictions and things. Most scientists before Albert thought it was really none of their business anyway. How could anyone *explain* something like the Universe? Isaac Newton had had a go, but his theory (a Universe full of stars that goes on endlessly in space and eternally in time) turned out to have a few problems.

At the time there was no scientific reason to believe that the Universe hadn't been around for ever. In that case, there were only really two possible ways the Universe might be:

1 The stars might go on for ever in all directions. But the problem with this was that, with an infinite number of stars, there would be an infinite gravity-pull everywhere. But there isn't. So that left...

2 Although space went on for ever in all directions, the stars petered out after a few zillion miles. As Albert put it: 'The stellar Universe ought to be a finite island in the infinite ocean of space.' But Albert didn't like 2 either. He decided that over very long periods of time, the stars would drift away from one another. Because the Universe was supposed to have been knocking about for ever, there shouldn't be any stars left to see – they would have all have drifted out of sight by now.

But then Albert had an amazing, incredible, wonderful idea. He already knew that matter – like a star for instance – curved space. So what would happen if there were dozens or hundreds or millions of stars? Space would curve more and more and more and more and more until...

Until what?

Well, until it closed in on itself. That would mean that although you could travel for ever and not find an edge to the Universe, you would eventually run out of new bits to see, and a light ray sent out into space would go round the Universe and eventually come back to its starting point. So perhaps you could see the back of your head zillions of miles away in space (if your head had a massive light bulb stuck to it).

Using General Relativity, Albert worked out an equation that described the shape of ... THE WHOLE UNIVERSE.

But there was a little problem...

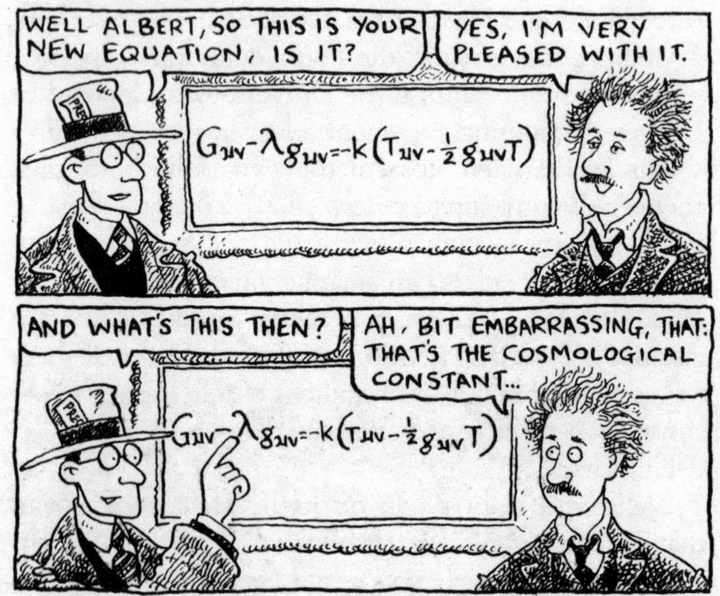

The cosmological constant was a thing Albert had to put into his equation for it to make sense. Because of the pull of gravity, stars attract each other as if they're connected with bits of stretched elastic. Imagine you're wearing an elastic tie, stretched to its limit, with a custard pie at the end. (If you haven't done this already, it just shows how uncool you are: make yourself one immediately. Then not only will you be stylish, you'll have a model of the Universe round your neck too.)

Now, pull the pie way from you. The tie will stretch and try to pull the pie back. All that stops it is your arm, pushing the pie away.

In Albert's theory, the pie is like one star, your face is another and the elastic is gravity. The cosmological constant is your arm. What would happen to the Universe if there was no cosmological constant? Try taking your arm away to find out.

So Albert's constant was very handy for stopping the Universe collapsing.

But it was a bit unsatisfactory for Albert, because there was no other reason to have the constant there. It would have been simpler to leave it out, and for Albert, simplicity was what science was all about. Still, he couldn't think of a way round the constant, so there it stayed for the next twelve years.

The retreating galaxies

Then in 1929, along came an American astronomer called Edwin Hubble. Edwin spent his time looking at galaxies to see what they were up to. And it always seemed to be the same thing – going away. Almost as if...

Albert's equations had always shown that the Universe was inflatable (and deflatable), but he'd assumed that it wasn't in fact doing either – because there was no

evidence to suggest it was. But now Hubble had found new evidence, that proved that it was actually inflating.

Again, it's like the pie on the elastic tie. There *is* a way you can stop it hitting you in the face. You can

throw it away from you. It will hit you later on of course, but meanwhile you can have a rest from all that pushing.

Until recently, it seemed the Universe is like this – that it is expanding at the moment, but that gravity will eventually win and snap it all back together again. Now it seems that the Universe has been thrown apart so hard that it will never collapse again – which is like throwing the pie so hard you snap your tie.

So that seemed to be that. The cosmological constant was all a big mistake. Perhaps. Recently, scientists have found evidence that actually the galaxies *are* moving as if there is a force like the cosmological constant pushing them apart.

Anyway, although cosmology has come a long way since Albert, it's still based on his original approach. As Elsa said when she was shown round a *massive* telescope in California and told it was used to find out the shape of the Universe:

NEW! FUN-SIZE

EINSTEIN'S EINCREDIBLE THEORIES
THE UNIVERSE

Albert used General Relativity to explore the whole Universe. But there were problems at infinity – so, being a genius, Albert did away with infinity with the stunning idea that the Universe is 'closed'. In a closed Universe you can travel forever without coming to an edge – but you will run out of new places to go. (Just as, however far you go on holiday, you'll never fall off the edge of the Earth – but you will eventually run out of new holiday destinations.)

Using the idea that matter curves space, Albert worked out equations that describe the whole Universe. But he ran into a problem. The stars, attracted by each other's gravity, would all rush together and the Universe would collapse. Albert suggested that there was a mysterious force that pushed the stars away from one another and stopped this collapse happening.

Many years later Edwin Hubble showed that the Universe was expanding, so there was no need for Albert's mysterious force.

(Though now it seems it just might exist after all!)

ALBERT AND THE NAZIS

In 1930 the Nazi Party received enough votes to get some real political power to back up their hatred of the Jews. But at this stage Albert – like lots of others – didn't take it too seriously. It was probably just as well that he went back to America that year, though.

On this second visit, people were even more bonkers about Albert than last time. Everyone demanded photos, interviews and signatures. Albert quite liked it and it did a lot of good too: Elsa made sure that every interviewer or photographer paid a fee, which went to the poor in Berlin and to people all over the world who refused military service. Albert also used the publicity to get people to listen to his views on pacifism – he said that if just two per cent of people refused military service, governments would be unable to make war. Whether or not this was

true, it sounded great, and lots of young Americans made themselves badges saying '2%'.

When Albert returned to Germany he continued to fight for pacifism and encourage people to refuse military service. Things were getting dangerous there by now, as the Nazis gained more and more power. And it wasn't just Jews they hated – they didn't like gypsies, gay people, people with mental or physical problems, or clever people like Albert either. Elsa said Albert should keep a low profile, but he said: 'If I did that, I wouldn't be Albert Einstein.' Instead he was about as political as he could be.

Before long, Albert returned to America yet again. While he was there he met a very rich bloke called Abraham Flexner. Abraham had $5 million to spend on a research institute and he wanted Albert to be part of it. It sounded great to Albert, and, not surprisingly, it didn't take too much persuading for him to decide not to return to Germany, especially when he heard that his house had been broken into to look for weapons. So Albert handed back the German passport he'd got when he arrived in Berlin, left the Prussian Academy of Sciences, and tried to warn people about the Nazis.

The Nazis hated Albert as much as he hated them. They told the Prussian Academy to expel him and were extremely irritated to find that he'd beaten them to it by resigning. Instead they insisted that the Academy issue an anti-Albert notice. They also seized all his bank accounts in Berlin, ransacked his flat, and even burnt his books.

The secretary of the Prussian Academy did as he was ordered, issuing a statement saying that Albert said the Nazis were cruel (a bit like saying poison is bad for you). Albert protested to Max Planck, who was a member of the Academy, but although Max was opposed to the Nazis' terror tactics he said he thought Albert's pacifism was just as bad. On the other hand, Max wrote a report for the Academy saying that Albert was as clever as Isaac Newton – and he and Albert remained friends.

Albert soon returned to Europe, though not to Germany. Among other places, he went to Belgium. He'd made friends with the Queen there in 1929, when he attended one of Solvay's conferences. He got on very well with her and the King, chatting together, playing string trios (with the Queen as the second violinist) and having fried eggs for tea. He always referred to them as 'The Royals'.

Then, one day in 1933, while Albert was still in Belgium...

Albert met secretly with the King, who told him what the problem was – some Belgians who had done what Albert suggested and refused military service had been put in prison, and they wanted Albert to speak on their behalf. The King was worried Albert would do this – it was less that three years since his 'two per cent' speech – and he was equally worried it would stir up trouble. As a personal favour, he asked Albert not to support them.

Albert wouldn't have done this as a favour to a mate – to him, individuals, even friends, were always less important than people in general. But the rise of the Nazis had made Albert think again about his idea that violence was never the way to solve a problem. Reluctantly, he now realized that sometimes there was no other answer, and that this was one of those times.

He did what the King wanted and didn't stand up for the prisoners. Although Albert fought hard for world peace for the rest of his life, he was no longer sure that it was possible without force.

Cloak and dagger

It was all very exciting for Albert round then – a bit *too* exciting for someone who wanted to be left in peace to solve the mysteries of time and space. Belgium is next to Germany, and it would have been easy for the Nazis to do what they wanted and arrange for Albert to be assassinated. The Belgian government gave two policemen the job of protecting Albert, and they asked the people of the village where he was staying to pretend never to have heard of him. But this didn't work too well and anyone who wanted to visit Albert had no trouble finding out where he was. When they got close to Albert's house, they tended to be jumped on by the policemen and sometimes Elsa would have to go out and rescue ambushed guests.

It's said that the Nazis also tried to get Albert into trouble by sending secret agents to see him. The agents pretended to be anti-Nazis and tried to get Albert to help them by smuggling weapons. They hoped they could then expose him as an unpatriotic German (they didn't know he wasn't German any more). Albert was a bit vague when he was busy thinking about science (he once set off for an important meeting, got lost, and phoned Elsa to ask 'where am I and where am I supposed to be?') but when he applied his mind to problems like the Nazi agents, he easily outwitted them.

Albert soon got tired of all this and went back to America, staying for a month in England on the way. While he was there he gave a lecture to an audience of ten thousand, including lots of scientists, plenty of politicians, and more than a thousand students and police who were there to protect him. Albert told them how dangerous the Nazis were. He also recommended putting brainy students in lighthouses so they could concentrate on physics!

After that, Albert left Europe for ever. He went to Princeton in the United States where Abraham Flexner had now set up the Institute for Advanced Studies he'd talked to Albert about before. The Institute was stuffed to busting with top scientists. In one of the main halls, a remark of Albert's had been engraved on the wall. Luckily it wasn't anything embarrassing like 'Down with socks.'

The Lord God is subtle, but malicious He is not.

Which is what Albert said to Dayton Miller (see page 125) when Dayton thought he'd proved that relativity was all wrong.

Albert loved the Institute, and Princeton, and at last he had the peace and quiet he needed to do his work – he soon found that all he had to do was be a little bit rude to people to get himself ignored. He worked away there quite happily with Elsa, his secretary Helen Dukas, a dog called Chico, a cat called Tiger and a violin called Lina.

The only problem was, now Abraham had his top scientist where he wanted him, he didn't want Albert to do anything but science – he especially didn't want him to do anything political. So he started to open Albert's letters and tell people who wanted to meet Albert that he wouldn't see them. Not surprisingly, this really got on Albert's nerves. When Abraham turned down an invitation from the US President on Albert's behalf, Albert had had enough. He made a huge fuss and threatened to leave. And he *did* go and have dinner with the President, so there. After that, Abraham left him alone.

Albert was having lots of rows just about then with just about everyone, and not only about being allowed to open his own letters. Most of them were about a theory he'd helped to invent. To tell the whole story, we have to go back to 1905 again.

LUMPY LIGHT

In 1905, Albert knew he'd come up with a really amazing and revolutionary theory. It was so amazing he got a Nobel Prize for it, yet it took twenty years until most scientists believed he was right. But the theory wasn't to do with relativity: it was all about light.

Brain Box

Atoms, energy, light and radiation
Atoms are mostly nothing with a hard bit in the middle. If an atom of, say, oxygen, was as big as the Earth, the bit in the middle (called the nucleus) would only be 100 metres across. The rest of an oxygen atom is empty except for eight tiny things called electrons. If the atom gets zapped with a light-ray, the electrons jump about, and they can even jump out of the atom.

Energy is the thing you need to do anything: open a cupboard, strike a match, prepare a Pot Noodle.

Heat, sound and movement are all forms of energy.
Another form of energy is radiation. Light is one type of radiation, but there are other types (radio-waves that you tune into to watch Star Trek, infra-red rays which you can feel as heat, microwaves to heat up your burger, ultraviolet rays that give you a sun-tan, X-rays that go through you and gamma rays that kill you).

A long time before Albert arrived on the scene, Isaac Newton had decided that light travelled in little lumps. But everyone was soon sure Isaac was wrong for a change and that light was really a wave.

The wave idea explained almost all the things that light does. But there were a couple of problems.

For a start there was a basic problem in thinking of light as a wave. Sound waves travel through air, and if you took the air away you couldn't hear anything, partly because you'd be dead but also because there wouldn't be anything to hear. It's just like what happens to sea-waves if you take the sea away. After all, a wave is just a wobble, and you can't have a wobble without something to do the wobbling. Trying to make a sound wave without any air is like teaching a snake to juggle.

So, if light was a wave, what was doing the waving? It couldn't be the air, because it was known that light could travel through glass jars from which the air had been pumped, and anyway there's no air between the Earth and the stars, but that doesn't stop you seeing them very nicely if it's night and not too cloudy.

Scientists decided that light must travel in *something*, and they called the thing 'ether' and tried to find out about it. They discovered that it was invisible, it didn't weigh anything, and sound couldn't travel through it. You couldn't breath it or smell it or taste it. And all the planets and stars were zooming about through it as if it wasn't there – it didn't slow them down at all. So what did scientists really know about it? After a few centuries, they'd come up with...

The second problem with thinking of light as waves was something called the photoelectric effect. Basically, as people in Albert's time knew, it's simple enough: light shines on a material like tin and the energy of the light knocks electrons out of it. The electrons are only held loosely in place in the tin atoms, and given a smallish zap of energy they can escape. And they can get this energy from light. The funny thing is that not just any old light will do the trick – for certain materials like titanium and uranium red light won't, but blue will. This is a strange thing to discover – it's like finding that blue things are always heavier than red ones.

What is the difference between red and blue light? Only that blue light waves are shorter than red ones. Now, if a wave is shorter it's more powerful: if you flap your hand about in the bath slowly you make long waves (like red light) but if you move your hand faster you get shorter waves (like blue light). Moving your hand faster takes more effort – more energy – so shorter waves mean higher energy. So there seems to be a sort of explanation here: blue light has more energy so it can knock electrons more easily.

But does this really make sense? If your bath is full and you want to give the water enough energy to escape, you could wave your hand about quickly and lots of little waves would overflow. If you moved your hand more slowly the water waves would still overflow, though it would take longer to get the floor properly wet. The energy takes longer to get there, but it gets there. So red light should eventually give the electrons enough energy to escape – but this never happens. You

could shine red light on titanium forever and not free any electrons.

When Albert applied his brilliant brain to the photoelectric effect, he soon found it was like the contraction of moving objects – the effects became quite natural and obvious once he looked at the Universe in a simpler way than common sense suggested.

What colour is black?

There was half an explanation around already, thought up by none other than Albert's mate, Max Planck. Max had been faced with a tricky problem, called the Black Body problem. Now 'black body' is one of the most unhelpful names in physics. What colour do you reckon black bodies are? Black? Nope; they can be red or yellow or orange or, very often, white. A 'black' body is something which shines with all colours at once. The amounts of these different colours depend on the temperature. Cool black bodies really are black, but hot ones give out a lot of red light and not much of any other colour, so they look red. Hotter ones give out more orange and yellow light, and very hot ones give out plenty of every colour, so they are white.

There are lots of black bodies in the Universe – including the Sun and the stars. And what's really handy is that there's a nice equation that says how much of each colour is present in a black body: the amounts only depend on the temperature. The equation is very useful – for finding out how hot stars are, for instance. But could anyone *explain* it? Scientists tried and tried and tried until they were sick, but they couldn't do it. Some of their equations predicted that black bodies would give out bursts of death rays, but luckily they didn't.

Finally Max came up with an idea – in some weird way, radiation from a black body behaved as though it was generated by little wobbly things on the body. The things could only wobble at certain exact speeds. Max didn't really think there were wobbly things (which he called harmonic oscillators or resonators), but he found that, if he pretended there were, he could do some sums and come up with the equation he wanted.

Brilliant. But irritating. Max hated his own idea and spent ages trying to prove it was wrong, but neither he nor anyone else could explain black body radiation without the wobbly things. Little did Max know that he'd just invented a whole new area of science that was to be called quantum theory.

Everyone else hated this idea too. Well, almost everyone...

ALBERT'S LOST NOTEBOOK

I love this wobbly idea. I'm sure the wobbly things are real. In fact... What if light is made of them?

Albert's little wobbly lumps of energy were eventually named photons (he called them light quanta). What we call the wavelength of light is just a measure of the wobbliness of the photons, and that means it's a measure of their energy – red light is made of slowly wobbling low energy photons, while blue light is made of rapidly wobbling high-energy photons. Photons are very small – a single star hits you in the eye with hundreds each second.

Albert's idea was extremely handy:

ALBERT'S LOST NOTEBOOK

HOW IT WORKS: THE PHOTOELECTRIC EFFECT.

How, for some materials, can blue photons eject electrons when red ones can't manage it?

Because red light is made of low-energy wobbly lumps. If one hits a piece of the material, it will transfer its energy to an electron, but it's not enough to eject the electron, which will just lose the energy again. But blue light has higher-energy lumps – each energetic enough to eject an electron.

It's like trying to kick a ball out of a ditch – you can give it as many little kicks as you like, it will just jump up a bit and roll down again. One really big kick, though, will be enough to get it right out of the ditch.

This way of looking at light led to the invention of TV: little guns fire electrons at special material on a television screen, and knock out photons from it. The photons then put themselves together into a nice picture of Captain Picard or Dot Cotton.

Albert's lumpy light idea also meant there was no need to believe in the ether any more: if light isn't simply a wave, it doesn't need anything to travel in. What a relief.

Isaac Newton thought light was lumpy and there was no ether too, so he would have agreed with Albert – up to a point: Albert found that the lumps *do* behave like waves in some ways. It's a bit like what he showed about time and space – common sense ideas don't make sense when they are applied to unfamiliar things – very very small things (like electrons), very very heavy things (like black holes) or very very fast things (like muons).

Just to put the tin hat on it, having shown that light can behave as lumps, Albert's theory – in the hands of a scientist called Louis de Broglie – suggested that electrons and other particles (which people had always thought of as lumps) can behave as waves.

Albert used his new 'quantum' ideas to explain all sorts of things, like the odd behaviour of diamonds at low temperatures. Meanwhile, a scientist called Niels Bohr used Albert's ideas to explain what goes on in the outer bits of atoms, the bits where the electrons whiz about...

Sodium street lights look orange. If we had eyes that could see incredibly tiny differences in colour, we'd see that this orange is very different to the orange of, say, an orange. The orange of an orange contains all sorts of different shades of orange, with yellows and reds too, all mixed up, but light from hot sodium gas contains just two shades of orange, very similar to each other. Other hot gases are like this – they give out light of only certain, exact colours. Niels explained why.

Heating something up means putting more energy into it. This energy is taken up partly by the electrons. As their energy increases they move further from the middle of the atom. But Niels realized that the electrons can't go just anywhere – they can only exist at certain distances from the middle of the atom.

After a while, the electrons fall down again. The energy they had, they give up as light – a single photon[1] per electron. Because all sodium atoms are the same, the positions the electrons fall from and to will be the same too – and so will the energy of the photons they give out. The colour of a photon only depends on its energy, so that's why hot sodium gas is always exactly the same orange.

1 Niels didn't talk about photons at the time – like most scientists, he didn't like the idea of light being made of little bits and preferred to think of it as a nice continuous wavy kind of thing.

Albert discovered an amazing thing connected with this. If there are lots of atoms of the same type, each with an electron at a high energy level, then the photon released when one of the electrons falls back will make the electrons in all the other atoms fall too, and release their photons all together, as a powerful pulse of light of an exact colour. This is how lasers work – so you could say Albert invented them, even though the first one didn't appear until 1960.

NEW! FUN-SIZE

EINSTEIN'S EINCREDIBLE THEORIES: PHOTONS

Max Planck could only explain the way objects change colour when they get hot by saying they must have wobbly things on their surfaces, which could only accept energy (from light, for instance) in lumps. He then spent years trying to prove the things didn't exist. Albert thought it made sense that light was made of lumps (now called photons) in the first place.

Albert and his friends discovered that light, electrons and other particles all behave as if they were lumps in some ways and waves in others.

Albert liked his theory, but there was one thing he was a bit uneasy about. If you've got an energized atom, you can't predict just *when* it will radiate its photon. As Albert said, 'There seems to be no "cause".' But in Albert's view of the God-like Universe, everything had to have a cause. This little worry was to come back to haunt him in a big way.

After this, Albert left quantum mechanics alone for a bit. When he came back to it he wasn't happy with what he found. Not happy at all.

The unreal world

The picture Albert had of the Universe at a tiny scale was of little lumps of matter (atoms), and little lumps of light (photons). It wasn't a lot different to the picture Isaac Newton had, but Albert had come up with a clear mathematical explanation of how photons and atoms worked. For Albert, that was all that quantum theory meant – that light, as well as matter, was lumpy. The lumps could behave like waves, but other than that there was nothing mysterious about them.

But, using the ideas of Albert, as well as those of Max Planck and others, younger scientists came up with a theory that explained all sorts of things incredibly well, but which went much further than Albert had.

What the new quantum theory said was:

What this means is, you can't *exactly* pin something down and say where it is at a particular moment, how much energy it's got and how fast it's moving. For big things this uncertainty is so incredibly small it doesn't matter, but for little things like electrons or photons it does. For instance, say you want to plot the path of an electron, finding out exactly where it is every nanosecond. You can't do it. You can never make an accurate measurement of the electron's path. If you try, your measuring instrument will disturb the electron, and change its speed and position. This isn't too surprising – but the new quantum physicists didn't just say you couldn't *measure* the exact speed and position of something. They said...

Then there are atomic processes like radioactive decay. Some atoms are a bit unstable and sometimes things just get too much for them and they go BANG. But no one can predict exactly when a particular atom will do this. Albert was sure that there *was* a reason that an atom fell apart at a particular time, even if that reason was unknown. But the new quantum physicists said...

And the new quantum theory said something even stranger: some things aren't really 'real' until someone measures them.

Imagine spinning a coin on a table and asking: 'Heads or tails?' While the coin is spinning, it's a daft question – the coin is neither. The only way you can get any sort of answer is to 'measure' the coin, but to do that you have to slap it on the table. But then, not only have you changed the whole situation (you've got a sad flat coin instead of a happy spinning one), you've also *forced* the coin to be a head (or a tail). And you can't predict the answer before you slap the coin, and if you do exactly the same experiment again, you're as likely as not to get a different result.

This is just like measuring what scientists call the 'spin' of a particle. Until you measure it, the particle hasn't 'decided' which way it's spinning. You can measure the particle, but only by adding so much energy to it that you change the whole situation, and force the particle into a particular way of spinning: measuring something as tiny as a particle is as violent as slapping a spinning coin. And you can't predict which way it will spin, and if you did exactly the same experiment again, you may well get a different answer.

So things like the spins of particles don't become real until the particles are measured. This is a very mind-blowing idea, especially to a scientist. Scientists had always thought of themselves like people watching TV, working out what was going on and predicting what would happen next. But the fact that they were watching made no difference to the programme: you can shout at Scooby Doo all you like, he still won't guess the ghost is really a burglar in disguise. But according to quantum theory scientists are more like the audience at a theatre. Throw a banana skin on stage and it will affect what's going on!

Quantum theory is strange, yet it's amazingly successful in explaining all sorts of things, like the way atoms absorb and radiate light. Today, just about the whole of chemistry only makes sense if quantum theory is true.

Quantum theory is really practical too. If an electron lurks about for a while at one side of a barrier which it doesn't have enough energy to break through, quantum theory says it will suddenly find itself at the other side! You can 'explain' this in various ways. For instance, you can say that it borrows the energy from nowhere or that it flips from one place to another without passing through the space in between. But however tricky it is to understand how the electron manages this, there's no doubt that it does: all sorts of equipment use an electronic device called a tunnel diode, which only works because electrons do 'tunnel' through 'impenetrable' barriers in this way.

Brain Box

Quantum theory

Quantum theory boils down to a few basic ideas:

- Light and particles behave as waves (in some ways).
- Light and particles behave as lumps (in some ways).
- There's a limit to how much you can find out about a particle.
- The Universe is fuzzy – that is, particles don't have exact speeds and positions.
- Sometimes, there is simply no reason why things happen as they do.
- Until a particle is measured, it hasn't 'decided' what it's doing.

What did Albert think of all that?

Albert had spent his whole life working out the reasons things happened. Now he was expected to believe that there was sometimes NO reason for something happening. He couldn't accept it, nor could he believe that some things are only real when they're measured. He thought quantum theory was brilliant and very useful, and he agreed that the Universe *looks* fuzzy and random – but he was sure that there were deeper secrets to be unlocked. Albert said that quantum theory…

…does not really bring us any nearer to the secret of the 'Old One'. I, at any rate, am convinced that He is not playing at dice.'

Albert spent the rest of his life trying to show that quantum theory had problems. This actually had a great effect on it – he was so clever that quantum scientists like Niels Bohr had to make their theories absolutely water-tight to escape him. Niels and Albert argued for years about it, in a matey kind of way, but neither could convince the other.

The quantum connection

One of Albert's last and most important ideas about quantum theory is still being argued about and experimented on to this day. In its modern form, it goes like this: many particles are formed in pairs, one spinning clockwise, the other anticlockwise (at which point they either separate or destroy each other). It's impossible for both particles to spin the same way.

Now, according to quantum theory a particle only 'decides' which way it's spinning when it's measured. So, once you've measured one particle and it's 'decided' to be spinning anticlockwise, the other particle has no choice but to spin clockwise – otherwise they'd both be spinning the same way, which is impossible. So, somehow, measuring one particle affects both of them! This must happen even if the particles are separated by trillions of trillions of kilometres. It's as if the particles are mysteriously linked, no matter how far apart they are.

Albert thought this was just so 'spooky' (as he put it) that it *couldn't* be true. But if it was false, then quantum theory must be wrong.

Albert's idea was too advanced to test until 1982, but experiments done since then have shown that particles really do behave in the spooky way the theory says – there *is* some mysterious instant link that connects them together. This seems to mean that everything in the Universe is mysteriously and instantly linked to everything else. Weird or what?

Maybe it's time to go back to Earth...

Albert and Elsa hadn't been in the United States for long when Elsa became ill. It was a terrible time for Albert, and he did all he could to help her, but after several months of medical treatment she died in their house at Princeton.

The news from Germany was equally depressing.

NEWS OF THE UNIVERSE

10 November 1938

JEWS PERSECUTED

Last night, Nazis arrested over 30,000 Jews in Germany. Seven thousand Jewish shops were wrecked, most Jewish churches burnt down and ninety Jews were murdered, while hundreds more were beaten up.

This is the latest in a series of anti-Jewish acts by the Nazi-controlled government – in 1933 Jews were barred from practising medicine or law and from teaching. In 1935 they had their German citizenship removed and earlier this year they were barred from many cinemas and theatres – and even from sitting on benches in many parks.

Albert helped people escape from this sort of persecution – by lending or giving them money for travel, and writing letters to make sure they were allowed to move to America. And when Albert ran out of money and the number of people trying to escape increased, he tried to organize more people to help.

Albert was convinced that the only way to solve problems like this for good was to do away with individual states and have a world government – with a peace-keeping army. But the US government didn't want the US to be done away with, thanks very much, and its national investigation service, the FBI, started to keep a close eye (and a big file) on Albert.

In 1939, Albert's sister Maja came to live with him. Now he was sixty he needed a bit of looking after: he was getting a little bit vague. One day, so it's said, he got lost *and* forgot his phone number – and directory enquiries wouldn't tell him what it was because he'd told them not to tell anyone.

A lot of scientists by now thought Albert had lost his way in physics too – Robert Oppenheimer said he was 'completely cuckoo'. Oppenheimer was one of the scientists who invented the atom bomb.

No. But he took the first step in its development, which takes us back to 1905 and Special Relativity again.

Fast means heavy

Albert had found that, as an object approaches the speed of light, strange things happen to time and space. The object gets shorter and clocks on it go slower. At the speed of light itself, clocks on board would stop and the object's length would be zero. But could anyone actually go that fast?

This isn't just a theoretical question. In laboratories all over the world tiny innocent particles are given enormous shoves – such hard shoves that, according to Isaac Newton, they should go much faster than light. Isaac would say that, if it takes a certain push to make a particle go at, say, 100 million metres per second, four times the push would make the particle go at 400 million metres per second. But Albert discovered this is impossible. *Nothing* can make the particle go faster than 300 million metres per second.

Imagine you want to test whether Albert is right. You have a little machine that can measure the speed of things, and you flick a grain of sand at the wall at 90%

of the speed of light (which is three million times faster than the fastest bowler ever bowled a ball). The sand grain makes a loud BANG when it hits the wall, and leaves a dent in it.

Now, say you flick it twice as hard. If you hadn't read the previous page, you might expect the grain to go at 180% the speed of light. But actually your little speed-measuring machine tells you it only goes at 97.2% the speed of light. But it does make a much louder BANG when it hits the wall. The wall shakes about a bit and a few cracks appear.

OK, so now imagine you try really hard and flick the sand grain twenty times harder than you did the first time. The machine will tell you you've still only managed to get the grain up to 99.97% the speed of light. But when it hits the wall...

If you didn't know better, you'd have thought the grain must have been going twenty times faster to do that. What's going on?

As everyone knows, things can hit hard either because they're fast, or because they're heavy. If you catch a ping-pong ball in one hand and a golf ball in the other, and both of them are going at the same speed, the golf ball will hit much harder. And that, Albert realized, was what happens to the energy you put into a thing to try to speed it up. The energy doesn't just go into speeding the thing up – it also makes it heavier.

Like the rest of relativity, this happens every day – whenever you throw something, some of your effort goes into making the thing heavier, and some to speeding it up. But at normal speeds there's only a really, really, *really* small increase in mass.

SCARY SCIENCE WARNING

Oops. Another equation. But you've seen it a couple of times before, nearly...

Here's the equation:

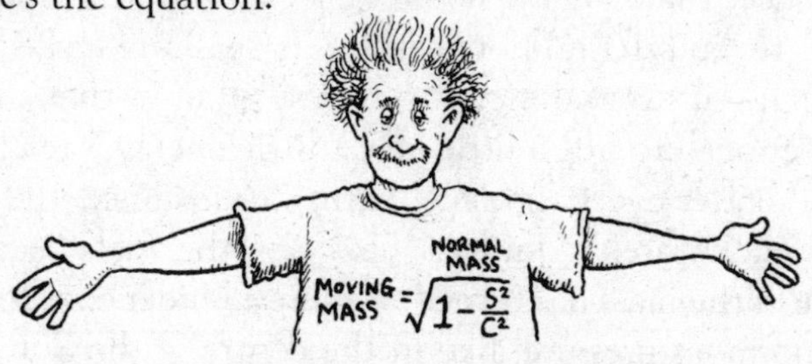

Looks familiar, doesn't it? And, just like the other things that happen in Special Relativity, this change in mass only happens according to people whom the object moves past. If you were moving with the object, you'd measure no change in its mass at all.

Albert discovered something amazing about mass and energy. In a paper only three sides long, he used relativity to explore what happens to a glowing object as it moves, and discovered a way of relating the energy of the glow to the mass of the object. His discovery applied to any energy (not just light) and any object (not just a moving one) and it led him to the most famous equation in the world:

Which means, to work out how much energy a particular object is equivalent to, you just multiply the mass of the object by the speed of light squared.

Because the speed of light is enormous, the square of the speed of light is incredibly big (to be strictly accurate, it's gob-smacking), so a tiny amount of matter has a gigantic amount of energy locked up in it. For instance, there's enough energy locked up in a grain of sand to boil 10 million kettles! It really *is* locked up though – it's very difficult to release all of it, though it's easy enough to free a little bit. A little energy is released from matter every time fuel burns, for instance: the ash and smoke aren't quite as heavy as the fuel, because some of the mass has turned to energy. Under conditions of enormous pressure, like in the centre of the Sun, it's possible to release a lot more of the locked-up energy, which is what makes the Sun shine.

On the other hand, energy can change into matter. This happens when sunlight falls on a growing plant. The light binds carbon dioxide and water together to make new bits of stick or banana, and the new bits are very slightly heavier than the carbon dioxide and water were. The extra weight is the locked-up energy of the sunlight. Burning (or eating) the plant will release the energy again.

In fact, all atomic reactions, all chemical changes, and all living processes only take place through the conversion of matter to energy and back again.

NEW! FUN-SIZE!

EINSTEIN'S EINCREDIBLE THEORIES: $E=MC^2$

The world's favourite equation says that matter is locked-up energy, and energy is matter set free. The c^2 bit shows that there is an ENORMOUS lot of energy in every bit of matter.

Albert and the bomb

So Albert had found that matter is locked-up energy. It was an incredible discovery, and $E = mc^2$ was the first step to atomic power, but there were a lot more steps left to take. Albert took just one more of them, in an article he wrote in 1920. He explained that lots of energy could be released from matter if the fragments of one broken atom were to smack into other atoms so hard that they broke too. Then the fragments of those atoms could break more atoms, and so on. This is called a chain reaction, and is just what happens in atomic power stations and atomic weapons. Chain reactions are like dominoes. You can set up a line of dominoes, knock the end one over, and all the others will fall too, like this:

But you could also arrange dominoes like this:

Then the first one will knock the next two over, which will knock the next four over, which will knock the next eight over ... until you've got dominoes falling over all over the place. A little bit like an atom bomb going off (but not very much).

But that was as far as Albert got. Even in 1935 he didn't think it would be possible to actually set off an atomic chain reaction.

So Albert had nothing really to do with the atomic bomb except for taking the first two steps. He might have had more to do with atomic science, if he hadn't had so much to do with atomic politics: to him the idea that people could one day release atomic energy was very bad news indeed, and he tried to stop it.

But there wasn't much he could do.

NEWS OF THE UNIVERSE

CENSORED

27 January 1939

ATOMS SMASHED

At a conference in Washington today, quantum boffin Niels Bohr announced that a colleague in Berlin had succeeded in smashing the atoms of a metal called uranium. A different substance – barium – was created and an enormous amount of energy was released. The conference speculated that an effect like this could be used to make an enormously powerful bomb.

These diagrams show the atomic chain reaction which takes place.

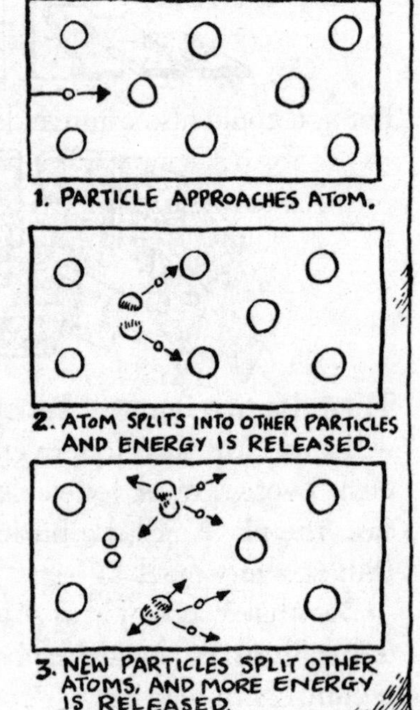

An atomic bomb was incredibly simple to make, once uranium of the right type had been prepared. A small lump would be highly radioactive, but it wouldn't explode – the atomic fragments would escape from it before they could crash into enough atoms to start a proper chain reaction. But if the lump was bigger than about 10cm…

In 1939, American scientists thought that the Germans were on the verge of making an atom bomb. They knew that uranium was the vital ingredient and that Germany had recently prevented Czechoslovakia from selling any to Russia. So two scientists went to see Albert, but not to ask for his scientific help – Albert was felt to be too untrustworthy for that (the FBI's file on him was 1,427 pages thick by then). They wanted Albert to pull some royal strings: Belgium owned more uranium than anyone else, and Albert's friends came to ask him to ask his old mate the Queen of Belgium (who was a Queen Mum by now) not to sell any to Germany.

After a lot of debate and pacing up and down, Albert ended up writing a letter, not to the Queen of Belgium but to the American President, Franklin Roosevelt. Albert said:

- It will soon be possible for a country to make atom bombs.
- Germany might be that country.

Though these things wouldn't have been secrets to Franklin anyway, the scientists hoped that the President would take them seriously if the world's top genius pointed them out to him.

Later that year...

NEWS OF THE UNIVERSE

3 September 1939

WAR AGAIN!

Following Germany's invasion of Poland two days ago, France and Britain today declared war on Germany. This follows the failure of negotiations to halt the advance of Germany through the Rhineland and Czechoslovakia.

Franklin wrote to Albert telling him that a research programme had been started to investigate nuclear power, and Albert wrote back, encouraging him to hurry it up.

Franklin started the top-secret 'Manhattan' atom bomb project in Los Alamos, New Mexico in 1941 – though more because of results from experiments than Albert's letters. Even though he wasn't told about the project, Albert probably knew what was going on because: a) lots of his friends were working on it; b) several of the atomic scientists that worked in his building disappeared; and c) he was a genius.

Why was Albert, who had until lately been opposed to all war and violence, so keen that the most powerful country in the world should develop a weapon with the power to kill millions? What he might have said is:

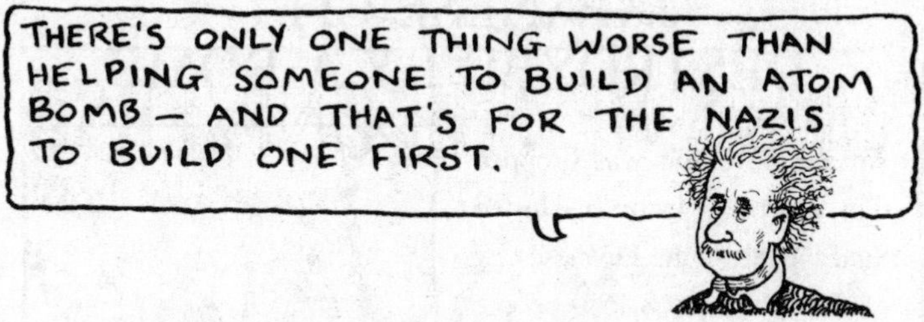

Also, Albert certainly wasn't opposed to *this* war. In fact he joined the US Navy to give advice on explosives, and helped the war effort by auctioning some of his old scientific papers.

But although Albert was convinced that the Nazis should be fought, and that it was vital to keep ahead of Germany in research into atom bombs, he was determined to stop them ever being used. So he wrote another letter, this time to Niels Bohr. In it, he urged Niels to help warn politicians about the dangers of atomic weapons. In fact, Niels had already started to do this – and was no longer trusted as a result.

Just when the Americans had a bomb ready, the tide of the war turned and it was realized that there was no atomic threat from Germany. But the atomic scientists were worried – they knew that America, having spent all that time and money on a bomb, would want to use it. They asked Albert to write to President Roosevelt again. Albert did, but by then Roosevelt was dead. And then it was too late. America was still at war with Japan, and, on August 6, 1945…

NEWS OF THE UNIVERSE

6 August 1945

JAPANESE CITY DESTROYED BY A-BOMB

An atomic bomb was dropped this morning from a United States plane on the Japanese city of Hiroshima. 78,150 people were killed instantly, and many more are likely to die from burns and the effects of radiation. An area six kilometres wide was flattened by the blast.

Albert was horrified. He'd even been to Hiroshima back in 1925.

Four days later…

NEWS OF THE UNIVERSE

10 August 1945

WAR IN EAST ENDS

Today the Emperor of Japan announced the surrender of his country, following the atomic bombs dropped on Hiroshima four days ago and on Nagasaki yesterday. After the surrender of Germany on 29 April, the Second World War is now at an end.

The war had killed more than fifty million people. Sixteen million people were slaughtered by the Nazis, just for being different: just for being Jewish, gay, a gypsy, mentally ill, socialist, Russian, Polish, Ukrainian ... Six million Jewish people were exterminated, two-thirds of all European Jews. The world was determined that there should never be another such war, and many thought that strong armies, armed with atomic weapons, were the only way to ensure peace.

Albert thought that was daft: atomic weapons would just lead to atomic wars, and the world wasn't safe while they were around. As he put it...

The war is won, but the peace is not.

To warn the world about this, he became chairman of the Emergency Committee of Atomic Scientists, which included scientists who had worked on the Manhattan project. But no one took much notice of them, and in 1948 the Committee broke up.

It was a bad year: Mileva died in Zurich, and Albert became ill again. He'd never looked after his health and now he had serious stomach problems. But Maja looked after him and, though he was never really well again, he kept working. He was so famous by now that he had endless visitors and letters from all over the world: including one asking whether he'd like to be President of Israel.

Meanwhile, research into atomic weapons continued. A new bomb was devised, a thousand times more powerful than the one dropped on Hiroshima. It was called a hydrogen bomb because it used an atomic blast to crush hydrogen atoms and produce an enormous amount of energy – the same process that makes the Sun shine. When Albert heard about this he appeared on TV to warn people that the development of the hydrogen bomb would make possible...

It was another bad time for Albert: not long after his broadcast Maja had a stroke and died. From then on, Albert shared his house with Helen Dukas, who had moved on from being his secretary to become his friend and housekeeper, and Margot, one of Elsa's daughters from her previous marriage.

By then, living in America wasn't much fun anyway: the Cold War had been going on ever since the Second World War finished. On one side was America and her allies and on the other the Union of Soviet Socialist Republics, which had been formed from Russia and neighbouring countries. The two sides were each battling against the political beliefs of the other, though without much actual fighting.

In America, a senator called Joseph McCarthy tried to find any Americans who supported Soviet ideas. That's what he said, anyway, but he was soon attacking anyone whom he decided wasn't a perfect American citizen, subjecting them to public interrogations. Albert openly criticized the powerful McCarthy and said that people should refuse to answer his questions, just as he would himself. He supported Robert Oppenheimer (the one who said Albert was 'completely cuckoo') too, when he was labelled as a security risk by the US government because of his objection to the development of the hydrogen bomb.

All this, combined with Albert's illness and frailty, might have made him very miserable indeed. But actually he was still doing what he loved best: developing amazing new science.

SUPERSCIENCE

Albert developed most of the science in this book between about 1905 and 1927. He died in 1955. What did he spend those last 28 years doing (apart from trying to save the world)? The answer would be amazing if you weren't used to Albert by now.

In 1928, Albert developed a heart condition which kept him in bed for four months. The enforced peace and quiet gave him time for plenty of thinking and, being Albert, the thinking wasn't about how he really must take more exercise or paint the ceiling. It was about a way of sorting out all the bits of the Universe he hadn't explained before.

ALBERT'S LOST NOTEBOOK

SORTING OUT THE UNIVERSE: THINGS TO DO.

Invent Special Relativity. ✓
Invent General Relativity. ✓
Help invent quantum theory. ✓
Measure atoms. ✓

Explain why the sky is blue.
Show that time and space are linked.
Buy oranges.
Show that matter and energy are really the same.
Show that matter and space are really the same.
Show that gravity and acceleration are really the same.
Show that electricity, magnetism and gravity are really the same.
Show that things aren't as vague as the quantum physicists say.

This wasn't the first time he'd wondered about such things – in fact he'd been puzzling over magnetism since he was five and his dad had given him a compass – and ever since he invented General Relativity he'd tried to stretch it to explain more about the Universe. But now he'd found a completely different approach, not just an extension of General Relativity, but something new.

When he was a young genius, Albert had been a bit scathing about mathematics – it was just a tool to fill in the details of his theories. But now it was the key to his new approach. He developed a whole new branch of it. A lesser scientist might have been satisfied to spend their life doing that, but for Albert it was just the start. He started to use his new mathematics to build model Universes, in the hope that one of them would turn out to behave like the real thing. If it did, the remaining mysteries of the Universe would be solved. There were two that Albert was especially keen to sort out:

ALBERT'S LOST NOTEBOOK.

1. Relativity theory shows that gravity is a curvature of space-time. But electricity and magnetism can't be explained like this. Wouldn't it be nice and simple if they could be? And couldn't we do away with the idea of matter entirely, and just talk about everything – atoms, gravity, apples, people – as if they were just twists in space-time? A Universe like this sounds so simple (and I've always believed the universe must be essentially simple).

2. The Universe can't really be all fuzzy and random like quantum theory says. There must be a better way!

Theories of everything

Because the theory would explain gravity fields, electric fields and magnetic fields all in one go, Albert called it a Unified Field Theory. Today a theory like this would be called a Theory of Everything, a set of equations that would contain *all* the science to explain the Universe.

Back in 1929, when he was still living in Germany, Albert had built himself a new house as a 50th birthday present. It was in a nice peaceful part of Berlin called Caputh, and it was there that he'd first tried his new plan, helped by a calculator called Walther.

No, no – they didn't have those then. Walther was a person who could do sums standing on his head.

The short answer is: No.

Over the years Albert thought he was near an answer several times, but it never quite worked. The problem was, he didn't have any single brilliant idea (like 'light is lumpy' or 'gravity disappears when you fall off a house') to help him this time. The nearest thing to this sort of idea came not from Albert but from a scientist called Theodor Kaluza who suggested that, if thinking of a four-dimensional space-time helped explain motion and gravity, adding a fifth dimension might explain everything else. Albert liked the idea and tried building it into his theory – but it didn't work. *Nothing* he tried during those 28 years really worked.

For many of those years, Albert was seriously ill, with intestinal problems and a swollen artery. In 1950, the artery began to get worse, and he knew he only had a little time left.

Albert was quite calm about the idea of dying, saying that it was...

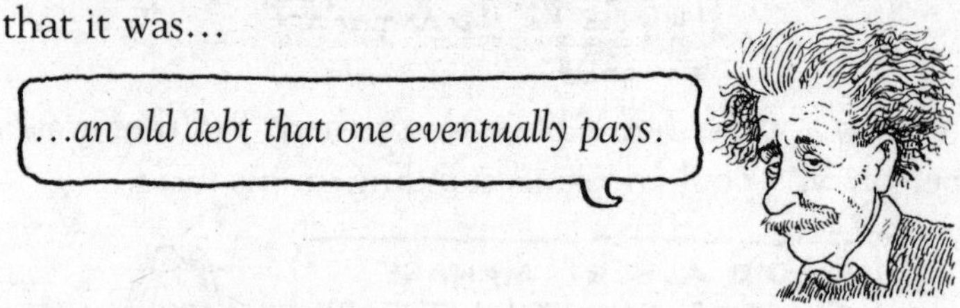

...an old debt that one eventually pays.

Although surgery might have prolonged his life a little, he refused it, and his last few years were spent working for peace and grappling with the Unified Field Theory, at home and at the Institute for Advanced Study.

On 11 April, 1955, Albert agreed to sign a protest against the international build-up of nuclear weapons. A few days later he was admitted to hospital as his condition worsened, but he continued working there, making his last calculations on Sunday April 17, 1955. He died early the following morning.

Maja, Mileva and Elsa had all died before Albert, but his sons survived him. Eduard had become mentally ill and had been living in a psychiatric hospital since 1933. He stayed there until his death in 1965. Hans Albert had a happier life. He became a Professor of Hydraulics at the University of California at Berkeley, and died in 1973. And perhaps Albert's daughter Lieserl survived him too.

Although Albert left his Unified Field Theory incomplete, his effort wasn't wasted. People are still working on Theories of Everything today, still using Albert's approach of building models of the Universe from pure mathematics, and still based on the idea of extra dimensions. But they still haven't got the theories quite right.

So what about Albert's two problems today?

1 The others are the strong force (which holds atoms together) and the weak force (which breaks particles apart).

The new, incomplete, Theories of Everything around today say:

Superstring theory says that everything is made of incredibly tiny things, much, much, much, *much* smaller than atoms, called strings. Some strings have their ends joined together, while others don't. And they all wobble about in different ways. Just to make it really complicated, strings don't just live in the four-dimensional space-time we know about. Their world has as many as ELEVEN dimensions (so Albert was on the right track when he tried exploring the fifth one). Seven of these dimensions are all scrunched up so we can't see them. The latest version of these theories, called M Theory, says that there are lots of other tiny things around too – little flat things and little lumpy squidgy things.

The idea is that everything can be explained in terms of these strings and things. Quantum theory, relativity, electricity, magnetism, you name it, the strings can explain it. String theory is nowhere near finished yet, and so far it's had one major success and one major problem.

The success happened when string scientists tried to make their job easier by not explaining everything at once. They knew gravity would be tricky, so they forgot about it, and just tried to explain the other forces they knew about. After they'd worked away for ages trying to get their incredibly complicated stringy mathematics to pull itself together and give them the force equations they wanted, they found they could more or less do it, but there were always some irritating stringy bits left over. However hard they tried, these leftovers kept cropping up. But when they looked at what these bits actually were, they realised that they were representations of gravity! It seems the theory does link gravity with the other forces, whether you want it to or not: so it *is* a Unified Field Theory, or it will be if it's ever finished.

The major problem is that there is no evidence that strings exist – they're far too small to see and there seems no way of doing experiments to prove they're real. Of course, this sort of problem wouldn't have bothered Albert at all – he'd just have come up with an amazingly simple idea, worked out the maths and then waited for the Universe to fit it. But superstring theory doesn't have an amazing Albert-type idea. Maybe it needs another Albert to come up with one.

It's not just in superstring theory that people are still using Albert's ideas: there's all sorts of work being done in cosmology and in astrophysics too, based on General Relativity. And, as for quantum theory...

Oh. Well, OK then...

As we already know, if you squeeze enough matter into a small enough space, you get a black hole. To begin with, a black hole doesn't seem very complicated – weird, scary, but basically simple – just something with really really strong gravity. But actually there's something very strange about a black hole.

Death stars

If it wasn't for the flow of energy from atomic reactions, any big star would collapse under its own weight, which is just what happens when its fuel supplies run out. The gravity is strong enough to crush not only its atoms, but even the particles the atoms are made of. By that stage, the gravity-pull is so strong that not even light can escape, so a black hole forms – and there's nothing to stop the star going on collapsing until it no longer occupies any space at all! This sort of thing is called a singularity, a place where strange things happen to space-time, things no one fully understands. But it seems that singularities may allow things to move backwards in time!

This is a very disturbing idea...

EXCELLENT! I'LL JUST NIP BACK AND STOP MY GREAT-GRANDPARENTS FALLING IN LOVE.
EASY TO ASSEMBLE (BATTERIES NOT INCLUDED)
ACME TIME MACHINE

THIS IS WHERE THEY FIRST MEET. GREAT-GRANDMA IS ON THE TRAIN AND GREAT-GRANDPA WILL GET ON THE SAME CARRIAGE. LET'S SEE WHAT I CAN DO ABOUT IT...

PLATFORM 1
W
GWR

PARDON ME, MISS, MAY I ENQUIRE WHETHER THIS COMPARTMENT IS FULLY OCCUPIED?
COR! SHE'S GREAT!
NO, INDEED, SIR, PRAY DO TAKE A SEAT...
COR! HE'S GREAT!
THE LADIES' EXCUSE ME LACROSSE
HEY MATE, YOUR HORSE IS ON FIRE!

THAT WAS FUN! NOW THEY WON'T MEET EACH OTHER, SO MY GRAN WILL NEVER BE BORN. AND THAT MEANS MY DAD WILL NEVER BE BORN EITHER. AND THAT MEANS...
RATS!
OH DEAR...
PHUT!

SINCE ERIC DOESN'T EXIST, HE DOESN'T GET TO INTERRUPT THE BEAUTIFUL MOMENT...
PLATFORM 1
G
W
GWR

PARDON ME, MISS, MAY I ENQUIRE WHETHER THIS COMPARTMENT IS FULLY OCCUPIED?
COR! SHE'S GREAT!
NO, INDEED, SIR, PRAY DO TAKE A SEAT...
COR! HE'S GREAT!

Weird isn't it? By going back in time you could change the past so you were never born. But then you wouldn't grow up – so you couldn't go back in time to change the past. So nothing would stop you being born. So you would grow up, go back in time and stop yourself being born. So you wouldn't grow up, go back in time...

If backwards time-travel is only possible inside black holes, it isn't all that interesting – no one can survive inside a black hole, let alone escape from it, so no one could really use one as a time-machine.

But scientists now think it's possible for a singularity to form *outside* a black hole – this would happen, for instance, if the hole is spinning fast enough. Then, to travel back in time you don't need to enter the black hole. You can just fly past it. If you're clever enough, you can leave earlier than you arrived (and then of course if you want you can stop yourself entering in the first place and get into the same sort of weird loop as if you upset your great-grandparents).

What does all this mean? Scientists aren't sure: it may be that General Relativity is wrong (but it's worked ever so well for donkey's years and there's no better theory available). Or perhaps there's some sort of 'fate' that would prevent you changing your own past (but that doesn't sound terribly scientific). Or it may really be possible, in some incredible way.

But spinning black holes aren't just a clever idea: there are lots of them scattered through the Universe, and it's possible that we'll find one that spins just right to act as a ready-made time-machine. And then where (and *when*) will we be?

Science has come a long way since Albert put it on the right track. Of all the thousands of millions of people who have ever lived, there are only a handful who achieved anything like the breakthroughs he did, and scientists agree that General Relativity is the greatest single theory ever created by a single person. After Albert died, people were so fascinated with his brain they took it out to have a look at it. To begin with it seemed just like anyone else's brain – grey, wrinkly, and not the sort of thing you'd want to find in your pocket.

But in 1996 scientists decided one part of it actually was a bit bigger than normal. But the way Albert used it to solve the mysteries of the Universe is really as mysterious as ever.

Albert was unique in combining his scientific work with a struggle for peace which inspired people all over the world. It's not surprising that Time Magazine decided in 1999 that he was 'Person of the Century'. Where Albert failed – in his work for peace and his search for a Theory of Everything – no one else has succeeded, and where he succeeded he completely changed our understanding of the Universe. No wonder he's dead famous.